Praise for *End Tim*

From the Rapture to the Second Coming to the Millennial Reign, there are a lot of complex topics in the world of eschatology. Jimmy Evans explains them with clarity and a deeply pastoral perspective.

Dr. Thomas Horn
SkyWatch TV CEO

Jimmy Evans penetrates today's culture with the timely truths of Bible prophecy. This book provides critical intel for hungry believers!

Jeff Kinley
Bestselling Author
Host of *The King Is Coming*
Cohost of *The Prophecy Pros* Podcast

In his landmark new book, *End Times Answers: 100 Real Questions from Real People*, Jimmy Evans, a leading prophetic voice and biblical scholar on the End Times, will provide the reader with solid, biblically sound explanations to 100 top (and at times controversial) questions circulating throughout the body of Christ. This is a must-read for anyone of any age searching for answers related to Bible prophecy.

Perry Stone, Jr.
International Evangelist

In his revelatory book, Jimmy Evans accurately addresses 100 of today's most poignant End Times questions. He skillfully speaks to both the scholarly and the laymen. In these last days this is truly a timely book for every man, woman, and child.

Bill Salus
Founder of Prophecy Depot Ministries
Author of *Psalm 83: The Missing Prophecy Revealed,*
How Israel Becomes the Next Mideast Superpower

I recommend this book to *anyone* seeking answers about the End Times. Jimmy's explanations are *powerful*, *balanced*, and *to the point*. This is a helpful resource that I will regularly recommend to people seeking biblical answers for the times in which we live.

Rick Renner
Pastor, Teacher, Author, and Broadcaster
Moscow, Russia

All of us pastors have heard the very real questions asked in this book, but few can answer as eloquently as Jimmy Evans. At a time when most End Times questions come from fear or anxiety, Jimmy's thoughtful, biblical answers offer hope.

Dr. Mark Hitchcock
Senior Pastor, Faith Bible Church, Edmond, OK
Research Professor of Bible Exposition, Dallas Theological Seminary

End Times Answers: 100 Real Questions from Real People is a very timely book with so many prophetically significant events happening today. Jimmy has done an excellent job of answering the questions and connecting the dots pertaining to prophecy, which is 27 percent of our Bible.

William Koenig
Koenig World Watch Daily
http://watch.org

When it comes to End Times discussions, people often think of it as doom and gloom. Yet the Bible calls it a blessing. That's what I appreciate about Jimmy Evans. He encourages us to get back to being a biblical blessing to a hurting world.

Billy Crone
Senior Pastor, Sunrise Bible Church, Las Vegas, NV
Founder, Get A Life Media

END TIMES ANSWERS

100 REAL QUESTIONS
FROM REAL PEOPLE

JIMMY EVANS

XO
PUBLISHING

TIPPING POINT
—— PRESS ——

ISBN: 978-0-9600831-5-2 Paperback
ISBN: 978-0-9600831-6-9 eBook

Tipping Point Press creates resources to help people understand biblical prophecy and the relevance of world events to the End Times. These messages provide hope, peace, and encouragement. For more resources visit XOMarriage.com or EndTimes.com.

Tipping Point Press, an imprint of XO Publishing
1021 Grace Lane
Southlake, TX 76092

While the author makes every effort to provide accurate URLs at the time of printing for external or third-party Internet websites, neither they nor the publisher assume any responsibility for changes or errors made after publication.

Printed in the United States of America

23 24 25 26—5 4 3 2 1

Table of Contents

Questions About ... Preparing
for Jesus' Return

Questions About ... Families and Children

Questions About ... Israel

Questions About ... The United States

Questions About ... The Church

Questions About ... The Third Temple

Questions About ... The Gog-Magog War

Questions About ... The Rapture

Questions About ... The Marriage Supper of the Lamb

Questions About ... The Tribulation and the Antichrist

Questions About ... Jesus' Second Coming and the Millennium

Questions About ... God's Final Triumph

Introduction

I have one word I will use to open this book: *gratitude*.

First, I am so grateful to God for letting me spend over five decades reading His Word and learning about what great things He has in store for *me and for all believers*. Sometimes in life, we do things that seem so inconsequential at the time, but then we look back and see the strong hand of God guiding us. For me, one moment like that was the day my wife, Karen, took me to a Christian bookstore to purchase my first Bible. I had never had a Bible of my own, and Karen wanted me to love the Bible as much as she does. That was also the day I purchased my first book about Bible prophecy, which was *The Late Great Planet Earth* by Hal Lindsey.

From that point forward, I started a habit of regularly searching the Bible for answers about the End Times. I've read hundreds of books about Bible prophecy, and I can't remember how many Bibles I have worn out over the years. I love God's Word so much that I can't imagine how anyone could live in this world without it.

When I became a pastor, I started preaching about the End Times and Bible prophecy. The more I preached, the more I realized three things:

1. Many people don't know a lot about Bible prophecy because they don't know what to look for in the Bible, or their churches don't teach much about it.

2. Many people are hungry for answers and want to learn everything they can about the future.

3. Many believers are unnecessarily frightened rather than comforted by End Times teaching.

For a long time, I have wanted to share the Bible's message about End Times prophecy with as many people as possible. It has been on my heart and in my prayers. In 2019, I began writing my first book on Bible prophecy. It was based on many things I had preached and taught about the End Times, but I also did a lot of research to add new content. In 2020, I was able to release that book, which is titled *Tipping Point: The End Is Here*. It has sold more copies in a shorter amount of time than any other book I have written. After *Tipping Point*, I wrote two more books about the End Times, called *Where Are the Missing People?* and *Look Up! Awaiting the Rapture and Our Final Redemption*.

As I was writing *Tipping Point*, God opened the door for our ministry to launch a new online presence for End Times Bible teaching and news commentary related to Bible prophecy. Every week, many thousands of people tune in to the *Tipping Point Show*. Since we began, many popular End Times authors, scholars and Bible teachers have joined us in fulfilling our mission, including Dr. Mark Hitchcock and many others. I have had many guests on the show to discuss various aspects of the End Times and current events. We want people to be informed, encouraged, and comforted, and we post new articles every week on our online newsletter. If you are not already a subscriber to endtimes.com, then please check it out. We would love for you to join us.

That brings me to the second thing I want to say I am grateful for: the subscribers to endtimes.com who regularly read our articles and watch the *Tipping Point Show*. If that is you, then *THANK YOU*. I can't imagine a more loving, supportive, and engaged group of believers. These subscribers faithfully watch the show every week. They pore over every article. One very popular feature of endtimes.com is the comments section where subscribers can ask and discuss questions. These subscribers have built such an amazing community of praying, Bible-loving saints. I know they pray for one another during times of difficulty, and I feel every prayer they lift up for me as well. I try to read as many of their discussions as I can, and I definitely see the light of Christ shining as I do. Again, I say *thank you* to these faithful friends.

From the very first episode of the *Tipping Point Show*, I have invited viewers to send in their questions about Bible prophecy and the End Times. I have received thousands of questions since then, and I have answered hundreds of them on my podcast. I wish we had time to answer every question, but this group of believers is so enthusiastic about seeking an understanding of what God is doing in these last days that I could answer questions 24 hours a day and still not get to all of them! If I ever wanted to find a group of Christians who love Bible prophecy as much as I do, I would not have to look far. They are right there on endtimes.com.

I decided to take some of the representative questions people ask and create a book to answer them. These are *real questions from real people.* I wanted to cover as broad an area as possible in terms of End Times prophecy. In some cases, I have combined questions because a similar question was asked by more than one person. In a few cases, I have used fictional names because we felt certain identities should be withheld in a written publication. However, these are all real questions that come from the people who watch the *Tipping Point Show.* If you asked one of these questions, I hope you will see how your love of Bible prophecy will help so many other people understand End Times teaching from God's Word. I consider you my colleagues in the process of creating this book. I pray God will give you a special blessing for walking alongside me.

I believe the answers in this book will inform, comfort, and encourage you. I hope you will take what you learn and tell others about the great plans God has for us. I believe our time before the Rapture is very short, and I am so happy you have chosen to learn everything you can about the wonderful future we have in Jesus Christ.

If you have never invited Jesus into your heart and life, I have included a very special section at the end of this book. I encourage you to read it if you are not sure that you are ready to meet Jesus when He comes again.

Special Instructions
Before Reading This Book

I have divided this book into sections that will make sense to readers. Most of the sections are in chronological order, and by that I mean they are in the order of how I believe things will happen from right now as we prepare for the Rapture until God's final triumph when we reach our destination with Jesus in the New Heaven and New Earth. I have pulled out some questions and put them into categories I hope readers will find helpful. For example, you will find sections on families and children, Israel, the United States, and the Church. The questions from those sections could have fit into a chronological pattern, but I grouped them together to help readers find them.

Also, I have answered each of these questions individually (one by one), so you need to be aware of two things:

1. You may see a term or phrase referenced in a particular answer that you don't understand, such as Rapture, Gog-Magog War, Armageddon, Antichrist, apostasy, etc. I encourage you to be patient because I promise that as you read through all the answers, these terms and phrases will be defined for you.

2. You will see repetition in some of the answers. I try to be as detailed as possible in each answer, and repetition will help you retain what you are reading. I want this book to be an educational resource for prophecy students, pastors, and leaders.

Questions About ...

Preparing for Jesus' Return

By far, the most questions we receive are about how to prepare for the Rapture when Jesus returns. People are understandably concerned about issues such as these:

- What the Bible says about the future
- How to know they are saved and will go with Jesus when He comes
- What kind of preparations they should make
- The chaos in the world right now
- How Christians should live in an unbelieving world
- How to witness to others about Jesus and things that are to come
- How they should pray for their families, churches, nation, and world.

These questions may seem overwhelming, but God doesn't leave us without answers. I always focus on what the Bible says about preparing for Jesus' return. God's Word gives us instruction, comfort, and hope. We don't have to be afraid. We only have to be ready.

1

What Still Has to Happen?

Based on the Bible's prophecy of things that will be fulfilled before the Rapture, what else do you believe is left that hasn't happened yet?

—Justin

In a word: *nothing.*

Based on my understanding of Bible prophecy, I don't believe anything else has to happen for the Rapture to take place. By the way, the Rapture refers to an event detailed in 1 Thessalonians chapter 4 when Jesus will return to instantly take His Church out of the earth to be with Him forever. This takes place just prior to the beginning of the seven-year Tribulation. Other answers in this book will give you more details about this.

As I've stated on the *Tipping Point Show*, I personally believe the Gog-Magog War—an attack on Israel prophesied in Ezekiel chapters 38–39—will coincide with or be very close to the time of the Rapture. And I believe it could happen very soon.

One reason I believe this is the way the Gog-Magog alliance is lining up. Notice how events related to Russia, Iran, and other nations mentioned in Ezekiel chapter 38 have been heating up in a big way over the past few years and months. It could be that between now and next fall something big could happen regarding the Gog-Magog War. That could coincide with Israel's Rosh Hashanah (the Feast of Trumpets), which I believe could be when Jesus comes to rapture His Church during that two-day festival. Again, you will find out more about this later in the book. But I also want to be clear that Jesus could come at any time, and we need to be ready at all times to meet Him.

I never set dates, and you need to be wary of any so-called prophet or preacher who claims to know exactly when Jesus will return. In Matthew 25:13, Jesus tells us that we won't know the day or the hour. But that doesn't mean we don't know the season and the signs of the End Times. Scripture clearly describes the broad timeline of the events of the last days. The Rapture is the next big prophetic event that will happen in our world.

The Bible does mention some things to look for prior to the Rapture:

- The return of Israel to her homeland (Deuteronomy 30:3; Ezekiel 36:24)
- False prophets and false Christs (Matthew 24:5, 11)
- Wars and rumors of wars (Matthew 24:6)
- Pestilences and earthquakes (Matthew 24:7)
- Birth pains/the beginning of sorrows (Matthew 24:8)
- Persecution of and hatred for believers (Matthew 24:9)
- Lawlessness (Matthew 24:12)
- The expansion of mission efforts around the world (Matthew 24:14)
- The great falling away or apostasy (2 Thessalonians 2:3)
- Perilous times and increasingly sinful society (2 Timothy 3:1).

You probably read that list and started checking all those things off in your mind.

We are living at a moment in which all the conditions seem to have been met for the fulfillment of Bible prophecy related to the Rapture of the Church. I don't believe there are any prophesied events that have to happen for that glorious event to occur.

But remember this: In Matthew's Gospel, Jesus said the timing of His return and the events of the last days are not for us to know or calculate with precision:

> Watch therefore, for you do not know what hour your Lord is coming. But know this, that if the master of the house had known what hour the thief would come, he would have watched and not allowed his house to be broken into. Therefore you also be ready, for the Son of Man is coming at an hour you do not expect (24:42–44).

We don't know exactly when the Rapture will take place, but we can be ready. Keep watch. Live as if the Rapture could take place at any moment, because according to the timeline in Scripture, it could.

2

What Should I Tell People?

Should I be telling people that I feel like the end of the age is near?

—Terry

I think this really depends on the person to whom you are talking. If you are talking to an unsaved person, then I would not necessarily recommend talking to them about End Times issues unless they ask about them. I would tell them about Jesus and what He has done in your life. I say this because if you start talking first about the end, then they might just think you're a nut and be turned off. It's not because what you are saying is nutty; it's because they only have a version of End Times teaching filtered through family, friends, the internet, or secular media. In some cases, they don't know anything at all.

However, once an unbeliever has an opportunity to understand who Jesus is and what He has done in your life, then they can see what He can do for them. Once they have accepted Jesus, then they are ready to learn more. At that time, they will need to hear about what the Bible says and understand that it talks a lot about the end, and *there is an end*. That is when you can tell someone what you believe and how the end could be very close.

I encourage you to use discernment. Pray a lot, read the Word a lot, and always listen to the Holy Spirit. For some people, it might be very appropriate to talk about the End Times. For other people, it might not be a helpful topic to address. But I wouldn't start with that when talking to lost people unless you feel as though the Lord is leading you. Our dear friend Rabbi Jonathan Cahn actually became a Christian by studying Bible prophecy. So, yes, there are some unbelievers who are open to discussing that topic.

However, we need to keep the focus as much as possible on Jesus and leading them to accept Him as their Lord and Savior.

Remember, witnessing is not just what we do—it is also *who we are*. As you witness to someone, you need to tell them what God has done in your life. Don't get involved in theological arguments with unbelievers, trying to convince them that they are wrong and you are right. I have found that fear, facts, and force seldom lead a person to change their mind. Hearing your testimony and allowing the Holy Spirit to work are what will bring people to Jesus. That is why when I witness to people, I just tell them about what God did in my life. No one can deny my experience. They might argue against theology, and they may say there is no God, but they can't deny how my life has changed. I profess that God did it, and I stand on that undeniable personal experience.

3

Is It Wrong to Predict?

For centuries people have tried to predict the coming of Christ, and they were wrong. I don't want to be chasing something that won't happen in my lifetime and then be disappointed. Do you think it is wrong for us to try and predict the Rapture? I know God gives us signs, but I still feel foolish trying to guess the time when so many have been wrong before.

—Sammy

Yes, I do believe it is wrong to set dates and be dogmatic about the timing of the Lord's return. However, I don't believe it's wrong to anticipate His return and be ready when it happens.

We have to be clear about one thing: Everyone who sets dates has ultimately been humiliated in the process. That's a quick way for a leader to lose credibility, and, yes, it does lead to disappointment and even cynicism when a predicted date comes and goes.

We ought to listen to what Jesus has to say:

Watch therefore, for you do not know what hour your Lord is coming. But know this, that if the master of the house had known what hour the thief would come, he would have watched and not allowed his house to be broken into. Therefore you also be ready, for the Son of Man is coming at an hour you do not expect (Matthew 24:42–44).

Notice Jesus did not say He was coming at a "season" we won't expect. He said it would be at an "hour" we don't expect. Believers must be ready at all times.

This is what the apostle Paul says about the matter:

But concerning the times and the seasons, brethren, you have no need that I should write to you. For you yourselves know perfectly that the day of the Lord so comes as a thief in the night. For when they say, "Peace and safety!" then sudden destruction comes upon them, as labor pains upon a pregnant woman. And they shall not escape. But you, brethren, are not in darkness, so that this Day should overtake you as a thief. You are all sons of light and sons of the day. We are not of the night nor of darkness. Therefore let us not sleep, as others *do*, but let us watch and be sober (1 Thessalonians 5:1–6).

When Paul says Jesus will come as "a thief in the night," that is a caution for unbelievers. The people who will not be ready for Jesus' coming are those who are unsaved and thus unprepared. That is why Paul tells Christians that the day of the Lord's return should not overcome them like a thief at night because we are "sons of light and sons of the day."

We are children of the light because we stay in the Word of God. We study Bible prophecy. We are observant, which means we can look at the state of our present world and *know* what we see now seems to match what the Bible says it will look like when Jesus returns. That is *right now*.

You will no doubt hear some people push against the idea that today's situation is unique. They'll say that every generation has had biblical signs of the End Times.

There is a lot of truth to this claim. There have been antichrist *types* in every generation—including public figures, such as Adolph Hitler, who believed and behaved in ways that completely contradicted God. These people were not *the* Antichrist, but they certainly did things that were against Christ. They had an antichrist spirit. Likewise, every generation has faced earthquakes, famines, and other signs Jesus spoke about.

But according to Jesus in Matthew 24:34, one generation at the end will see every sign. The most important sign that announced the beginning of the final generation was the reestablishment of Israel as a nation on May 14, 1948. That event fulfilled the prophecy of Isaiah 11:11–12 as well as many other prophecies in the Old Testament. The existence of Israel as a nation is the super-sign of the End Times and proof that we are living near the end of this age. I don't think it's wrong in any way for us to be watchful and prepared, especially in this current generation.

I don't think it's wrong for us to say the Rapture could happen at any moment.

No, I don't know the day Jesus is coming. I don't know the hour He's coming. But I certainly believe we are living within the *season* of His coming. There is nothing disappointing about that! Quite the opposite—it should give us hope!

4

Comfort or Urgency?

I'm very concerned for the unbelieving world. I love people and want to see them saved. How do I, as a follower of Christ, strike a balance between the comfort of being safe in Christ and the terrifying urgency of the coming judgment?

—Eric

I really appreciate the heart behind this question. First, I want you to know that all believers are going to Heaven. We know that because we have the promise that when Jesus comes in the Rapture, He will take us with Him. The apostle Paul makes this clear:

> Then we who are alive *and* remain shall be caught up together with them in the clouds to meet the Lord in the air. And thus we shall always be with the Lord. Therefore comfort one another with these words (1 Thessalonians 4:17–18).

It's worth noting that Paul wrote "comfort one another with these words." The concept of the Rapture should bring us comfort and peace because we, as believers, are going to Heaven with Jesus. There we will join Him in the great Marriage Supper of the Lamb.

But in the meantime, we also have the responsibility to preach the gospel and carry out the Great Commission (see Matthew 28:16–20). Jesus told us to go all over the world and make disciples of all nations.

Jesus also taught the Golden Rule: "Therefore, whatever you want men to do to you, do also to them, for this is the Law and the Prophets" (Matthew 7:12). If I were not a believer, then what would I need believers to do for me, even if I wasn't aware that I needed it? I would need for them to pray for me and try to reach me with the saving message of Jesus. For all of us, there is a balance

10

of comfort in our eternal destination and urgency to share about Jesus. It's understandable for Christians to feel that tension.

Nevertheless, some believers might be tempted simply to rest in comfort, which is really a sort of arrogance. They may think of themselves as exclusive and chosen by God. Jesus told a parable about a Pharisee who had that mindset:

> Also He spoke this parable to some who trusted in themselves that they were righteous, and despised others: "Two men went up to the temple to pray, one a Pharisee and the other a tax collector. The Pharisee stood and prayed thus with himself, 'God, I thank You that I am not like other men—extortioners, unjust, adulterers, or even as this tax collector. I fast twice a week; I give tithes of all that I possess.' And the tax collector, standing afar off, would not so much as raise *his* eyes to heaven, but beat his breast, saying, 'God, be merciful to me a sinner!' I tell you, this man went down to his house justified *rather* than the other; for everyone who exalts himself will be humbled, and he who humbles himself will be exalted" (Luke 18:9–14).

Don't fall into the trap of thinking, *Thank You, Lord, that I'm not like those bad sinners. They're really terrible people.* Jesus had some tough words about anyone who thinks that way.

Believers who feel this way may share the comfort other believers have in knowing that Jesus is coming, but at the same time, they aren't following Jesus' command to preach the Good News. There are also believers who haven't understood about the Rapture—so they don't have that comfort in the first place—and they also don't preach the gospel.

When I talk about "preaching the gospel," I mean two things:

1. Being willing to share our own personal testimonies with others about what Christ has done in our lives. This is commonly called "witnessing," and it terrifies a lot of believers because they fear failure and rejection. We must understand that witnessing isn't just what we do—it is also who we are. We are witnesses of what Jesus has done in our lives, and that is a powerful testimony to unbelievers who are open to God.

2. Preaching the gospel also means partnering with churches and ministries that are spreading the Good News of Jesus. This can mean financially supporting them, and it also means

serving in your church or in a ministry that helps people find Christ. You may feel as though you have never personally led a person to Christ. But if you have financially supported or served in a church or ministry that has led someone to Jesus, then you are certainly preaching the gospel.

As Christians, the best approach is balance. I believe there are some people who see the world as their enemy, while others see the world as their home. God wants us to see the world as our mission field. This is not our home, and people in the world are not our enemies. *Let's tell them about Jesus.*

And if we truly love people, then we need to be supporting our local churches and ministries that reach people. We also need to be sharing our testimonies. When you witness about Jesus, you're not trying to argue theology with anyone, because that can be intimidating for all of us.

We don't need to have every answer. We simply need to tell people what Jesus has done for us. You don't have to agree with my theology, but I can tell you this: My experience speaks for itself.

I was a mess, and then I met Jesus. He came into my life, touched me, and set me free. You can argue about theology all you want, but you can't argue with how God's power changed me and set me free! It is an undeniable fact. All I have to do is be willing to share it when I have the opportunity.

People don't need a bunch of theology; they just need someone who loves them enough to share the Good News of Jesus' love. And that's what we need to be doing as we see the stage being set for the return of the Lord.

5

How Should I Prepare?

What does it mean to be ready for when Jesus comes? Is there something we should be actively doing to prepare for the Rapture? How do we educate people who are not familiar with End Times prophecies?

—Jeffrey

First, I really do think endtimes.com is one of the best ways you can get encouragement and education about what is going to happen in the coming days. We don't focus our teachings on scaring anyone, because God's promises should be comforting. End Times prophecy should encourage and comfort you when you understand it. Every week, all week long, we are educating people.

Second, reading good books will help you. My books titled *Tipping Point, Where Are the Missing People?,* and *Look Up!* are all focused on education and encouragement. Dr. Mark Hitchcock has written over 30 great books on the End Times. Billy Crone, Dr. David Jeremiah, Rabbi Jonathan Cahn, Pastor John Hagee, Greg Laurie, and others will help you understand what is happening and what will happen in the future. All of these people are dispensational theologians, pastors, and teachers. That means we all believe in the literal interpretation of the Bible, unless the text is clearly allegorical. Sometimes the Bible includes allegory, but we don't try to allegorize passages when the plain meaning is literal.

Listening to good teachers and reading their books is what I did. I first started reading about Bible prophecy almost 50 years ago when I read Hal Lindsey's *The Late Great Planet Earth.* Then I read another book and another. I consumed everything I could get my hands on. Early on, I didn't know enough to stay away from bad authors, so I did read a few books with some terrible End Times theology in them. But by God's grace I continued to study, and some good authors helped me find the truth.

Third, while you are filling your mind, pay attention to your heart. Jesus said, "And because lawlessness will abound, the love of many will grow cold" (Matthew 24:12). We must understand that morality protects us. If you're a believer and also a moral and ethical person, then it means you are safe. You will be mannerly and honest. You won't try to take advantage of anyone. You will never try to harm others. On the other hand, an immoral person lies and steals. They will commit actions they know are not right and take no responsibility for the harm they cause. Lawlessness causes damage and mistrust. As a believer, you may be tempted to separate and protect yourself, and some of that is necessary. But don't let your heart become hard.

Unforgiveness causes our hearts to harden toward specific individuals and whole groups of people. When that happens, we become unforgiving to individuals, political parties, denominations, and certain types of Christians. It is easy to let your heart grow hard in the middle of injustice and lawlessness because of the hurts you witness in others or personally endure. I encourage you to say this prayer every day: *Lord, forgive me of my debts as I forgive my debtors.* Then be specific about those people who have offended you, those who have done wrong to you, and those who have harmed people you care about. Forgiveness tenderizes our hearts and keeps us softhearted toward each other.

I will give an example from my own life. I vote for people who are pro-life. This issue is the most important thing to me in any election. But what if a person is pro-abortion? I still love and pray for them, even when I don't agree with them. If someone stands against what I believe in politically and morally, then Karen and I both make it a habit to pray for those individuals. We pray for celebrities, politicians, and regular people because it is the right thing to do. It keeps our hearts soft. It will also keep you from becoming cynical and hardened, which is what I see in a lot of Christians these days. That's not the kind of people we are supposed to be as believers. We're supposed to be people of prayer and love. We don't compromise on the gospel, but that also means we are always praying for people who are not Christians to come to Jesus above all things.

Yes, we see rampant immorality, deception, violence, and lack of fear of the Lord. Even so, a righteous remnant still stands for God. This is where we are. These are the days in which we are living. We are only seconds from midnight prophetically, but that means we should be even more concerned for the lost around us. Our hearts need to remain soft so we will never stop telling others about God's love for them.

6

What Role Does the Feast of Trumpets Play?

I have heard you say you "always get serious" before the Feast of Trumpets because you believe Jesus will come during that festival. What does that mean? And are there certain things we need to do to be ready for the Rapture?
—Amanda

The best thing anyone can do to *get ready* for the Rapture is to *be ready* for it. When I say I "get serious," what I mean is that I get really focused. I believe that during the Feast of Trumpets some year, the Rapture could happen. I often talk about the Feast of Trumpets and all the symbolism surrounding it, and I personally believe that the fulfillment of that feast is the Rapture of the Church.

The Rapture can happen at any time. God doesn't follow our timetable, and Jesus doesn't have to have our permission to come. Christians should always be ready. What I don't want to do is promote an attitude that says we only need to focus on Jesus coming for the two days a year when the Feast of Trumpets happens and just do whatever we want the rest of the time. I don't live that way, and I don't believe that way.

However, there are a few things I do a little differently during the Feast of Trumpets. A day or two before the feast, my wife, Karen, and I pray and take communion together. We will ask the Lord to prepare our hearts to see Jesus. If we have any sins to confess, then we also do that. We try to confess our sins often, but this is one time we make sure we do it. This is a way we can say, "Come, Lord Jesus." We don't want to be doing anything we shouldn't when Jesus comes, but we are not afraid because we know Him. I know it is only by His grace that I am saved, but I want to be as pleasing to Him as I can be. I intentionally focus on the Lord and my relationship with Him.

I believe the seven feasts God gave to Israel are a prophetic grid of the future. We know Jesus was crucified during the Feast of Passover, buried during the Feast of Unleavened Bread, and resurrected during the Feast of First Fruits. The Holy Spirit fell on the Church during the Feast of Pentecost. We absolutely know when God gave Israel those feasts that He was showing them and us the future in advance. Every feast was fulfilled on the actual day by a massive, world-changing event. That's what happened during those first four feasts that occur in the spring, but remember, there are seven. Three more are coming, and they have to be fulfilled in order. These next three feasts occur in the fall of the year. The next feast in line for fulfillment is the Feast of Trumpets. It is celebrated in September or October of the year on the Gregorian calendar. I believe it will be fulfilled prophetically by the Rapture of the Church. The other two feasts—The Day of Atonement (Second Coming) and the seven-day Feast of Tabernacles (eternity with God)—will follow in successive order.

When the Rapture occurs along with Feast of Trumpets, I believe the Tribulation will begin shortly thereafter. There could be an interval of time between the Rapture and the beginning of the Tribulation, but I don't believe it will be very long. I believe Scripture strongly connects the Rapture and the Feast of Trumpets. I am not dogmatic about these things, but I do personally believe the Rapture will be a fulfillment of that feast. I want to show a couple of Scriptures that I believe confirm this position.

In 1 Thessalonians chapter 4, the apostle Paul says,

> For this we say to you by the word of the Lord, that we who are alive *and* remain until the coming of the Lord will by no means precede those who are asleep. For the Lord Himself will descend from heaven with a shout, with the voice of an archangel, **and with the trumpet of God.** And the dead in Christ will rise first (vv. 15–16, bold mine).

Then 1 Corinthians chapters 15, Paul writes the following:

> Now this I say, brethren, that flesh and blood cannot inherit the kingdom of God; nor does corruption inherit incorruption. Behold, I tell you a mystery: We shall not all sleep, but we shall all be changed—in

a moment, in the twinkling of an eye, **at the last trumpet. For the trumpet will sound**, and the dead will be raised incorruptible, and we shall be changed (vv. 50–52, bold mine).

Chapters 2 and 3 of the book of Revelation are Jesus' letters to the seven churches. This is how chapter 4 begins:

After these things I looked, and behold, a door *standing* open in heaven. And the first voice which I heard *was* **like a trumpet** speaking with me, saying, "**Come up here**, and I will show you things which must take place after this" (v. 1, bold mine).

Many Bible scholars believe this passage is about the Rapture. The Church Age ends after chapters 2 and 3, and the Rapture occurs in the very beginning of chapter 4. John hears a voice "like a trumpet" that says, "Come up here." Immediately, he is in the Lord's presence. I would also draw attention to chapters 6 through 18, which are an account of the Tribulation. The Church is never referenced in those chapters while it was referenced extensively before that. This is one of the evidences that points to the Church being raptured before the Tribulation, and I believe the beginning of chapter 4 is a reference to the Feast of Trumpets and the Rapture.

Consequently, I believe some year during the Feast of Trumpets, which is a two-day period in the fall of the year, the Rapture will happen. Again, people should be ready all the time. Those are not the only two days we should prepare to meet the Lord.

Historically, Jews have other ways of referring to the Feast of Trumpets. One of those is *Yom Teruah*, which means 'the day of the blowing' or 'the day of the awakening blast.' In 1 Thessalonians 4:16, which I referenced above, the Lord comes from Heaven with a shout and the blast of a trumpet, and the dead in Christ are resurrected.

Yom HaDin is another way to refer to the Feast of Trumpets, and it means 'the day of judgment.' In Revelation chapter 22, Jesus says,

And behold, I am coming quickly, and My reward *is* with Me, to give to every one according to his work. I am the Alpha and the Omega, *the* Beginning and *the* End, the First and the Last (vv. 12–13).

When Jesus comes in the Rapture, it will be a day of judgment. Believers will be judged based on our works. Jesus saves us by grace, but we are still judged based on our works.

Jews also refer to the Feast of Trumpets as the wedding day of the Messiah. When we are raptured, we will go to the Father's house. In John chapter 14, Jesus told His followers that He was leaving them to go to the Father's house, but He would come back to get them. In the meantime, He would prepare a place for them to be with Him. Jesus was using wedding language. A Jewish bridegroom would go back to his father's house and prepare a place for his bride. Then he would come back and get her.

So in John chapter 14, Jesus is saying, "I'm leaving. I'm going to prepare a place for you in My Father's house, and then I'm going to come back and get you to marry you." The Rapture is when we will be taken to the Father's house to spend seven years marrying Jesus. Then we will return with Him in the Second Coming at the end of the Tribulation (see Revelation chapter 19 and Zechariah chapter 14).

One more thing I will mention is that Jews have also referred to the coming of the Messiah as "the day which no one knows." If Jesus comes at the Feast of Trumpets, then it is the day which no one knows because it's a two-day feast. He could come on either day. In Mark chapter 13, Jesus said, "But of that day and hour no one knows, not even the angels in Heaven, nor the Son, but only the Father" (v. 32). If I told you that the Rapture would happen this year during Trumpets, you still would not know the day or the hour.

I believe there's a strong basis in Scripture and in the Jewish faith to expect that the Rapture will be fulfilled during the Feast of Trumpets. I believe the Second Coming after the Tribulation will be fulfilled on the Day of Atonement. Then I believe God's final triumph when we will spend eternity with Him will begin at the seven-day-long Feast of Tabernacles. I believe these events will soon be literally fulfilled. The next one to happen will be the Rapture at the Feast of Trumpets. If I am wrong at any point in my interpretation, then I still urge Christians always to be prepared for Jesus' return. I am certain about His soon return without any reservation.

7

Should I Quit My Job?

In Revelation, Jesus tells some of the churches He is upset with them because of their tolerance of sin or sinful people. In the secular workplace that's growing increasingly anti-Christian, should Christians consider leaving their jobs to avoid the tolerance Jesus warns about?

—Trey

I know this is an issue many believers are facing. However, the problem Jesus addresses in this passage of Revelation is tolerance toward sin *within* the church rather than people outside.

Let's look at what Jesus personally said to the church at Thyatira:

> I know your works, love, service, faith, and your patience; and *as* for your works, the last *are* more than the first. Nevertheless I have a few things against you, because you allow that woman Jezebel, who calls herself a prophetess, to teach and seduce My servants to commit sexual immorality and eat things sacrificed to idols. And I gave her time to repent of her sexual immorality, and she did not repent. Indeed I will cast her into a sickbed, and those who commit adultery with her into great tribulation, unless they repent of their deeds. I will kill her children with death, and all the churches shall know that I am He who searches the minds and hearts. And I will give to each one of you according to your works (Revelation 2:19–23).

Jesus is speaking to the Church *about* the Church. He's not talking about the workplace. He is saying that those who are in the Church have a responsibility to govern it according to God's standards.

Jesus was chastising the church at Thyatira for tolerating a woman *inside* the church who was teaching lies and actively leading people to commit sin. Every church is accountable to God for what they allow and what they forbid. And if sin is tolerated, then it will ultimately destroy the work of God in that place. This issue is rampant in the Church today, and it's the reason so many congregations are dwindling and even dying.

As for the workplace, let's say you work in a business that specializes in sin and vice, such as a strip club. Then you need get out because you would be participating in something you know harms people and is outside of God's will. The same would be true if you are working for a business or company that tries to force you to do something you know is sin or violates your conscience.

When I was in college, I worked in a car wash with some of my friends. The week before my wife, Karen, and I got married, I received Christ. When we got back from our honeymoon, I went back to work at the car wash, and could only stay for half a day because of how verbally filthy the environment was. As a new believer, I wasn't strong enough to endure it. Just two weeks earlier I was as dirty as any of them. But as a new Christian, I believe it was God's will for me to get out of that environment.

Shortly after that I went to work for my uncle in the appliance business. I was a delivery man for him and later for my father. I still worked around a lot of unbelievers (some of whom I eventually led to the Lord), but it was a better environment than the car wash, and I was growing in God. I don't believe it's reasonable or possible to try to find a sinless place to work. But I do believe sometimes the Lord might lead us to get out of a place for our own good.

Here's what Paul wrote to the church at Corinth:

> I wrote to you in my epistle not to keep company with sexually immoral people. Yet I certainly *did* not *mean* with the sexually immoral people of this world, or with the covetous, or extortioners, or idolaters, since then you would need to go out of the world. But now I have written to you not to keep company with anyone named a brother, who is sexually immoral, or covetous, or an idolater, or a reviler, or a drunkard, or an extortioner—not even to eat with such a person.
>
> For what *have* I *to do* with judging those also who are outside? Do you not judge those who are inside? But those who are outside God judges. Therefore "put away from yourselves the evil person" (1 Corinthians 5:9–13).

Paul was writing about a young man who was having sexual relations with his father's wife (the young man's stepmother). Paul told the Corinthian church that they must deal with this young man who was living in this kind of sin. The apostle said they would need to put him out of the church if he was unwilling to repent and stop his behavior. This is a church matter, through and through.

As for friendships and work colleagues, you need to have close friends around you who are believers. You need Christian friends—close friends—and you should try to have regular fellowship with them.

But when you go to work, it is almost impossible to avoid contact with unbelievers. Some will be Mormons, Muslims, atheists, or whatever else. Your task is to work with them and try to be a good influence on them. If you *are* going to be around unbelievers, however, you need to balance that with strong Christian fellowship, because unbelievers' ways of behaving can rub off on you. In 1 Corinthians 15:33, the apostle Paul said, "Don't be deceived: 'Bad company corrupts good morals'" (AMP).

We must remember what Jesus said about being "light" in the world:

> You are the light of the world. A city that is set on a hill cannot be hidden. Nor do they light a lamp and put it under a basket, but on a lampstand, and it gives light to all *who are* in the house. Let your light so shine before men, that they may see your good works and glorify your Father in heaven (Matthew 5:14–16).

With that Scripture in mind, use your workplace as an opportunity to let your light shine for those who are living in sin or spiritual darkness. Pray before you go to work and ask the Lord to give you strength and His special grace to love those around you and to see them through His eyes.

8

Is Revelation Chronological?

Is the book of Revelation a strict, chronological timeline, or are some portions in a different order?

—Terrence

Revelation is generally written in chronological order. What is recorded in the book spans over thousands of years—all the way back to the Old Testament. In the 404 verses of Revelation, there are hundreds of citations from or allusions to the Old Testament. The book begins in chapter **1** with "The Revelation of Jesus Christ." We see the glorified and eternal Son of God in Revelation in a way that He appears nowhere else in Scripture.

Chapters **2–3** contain Jesus' messages to the seven churches of Asia Minor, which is in modern-day Turkey. Those messages were to actual churches of the apostle John's day, but they are commonly believed by theologians to represent the Church Age from John's time until ours. We, therefore, are in the age of the church of Laodicea, which is the lukewarm, arrogant church that Jesus pled with to repent with the threat of spewing them out of His mouth. This isn't true of every church today, but it is true of most churches, especially in the West.

I believe chapters **4–5** of Revelation are a picture of the Rapture of the Church and our presence in the throne room of Heaven as Jesus, the Lamb of God, prepares to break the seals of the scroll to begin the seven-year Tribulation. The Seal Judgments occur in Revelation 6:1–8:5.

Chapters **6–18** of the book of Revelation describe the time of the seven-year Tribulation. In the middle of that description, in chapters **11–13**, there is a parenthetical section that chronicles mid-Tribulation events such as the death of the Two Witnesses, the rise of the Antichrist and False Prophet, the Abomination of Desolation, and other happenings.

The Tribulation is seven years long and is divided into two, three-and-a-half-year periods. The final three-and-a-half-year period is called the Great Tribulation because it is much more severe than the first half of the Tribulation. Some Bible scholars (with whom I agree and respect) believe the Seal Judgments happen during the first half of the Tribulation. The Abomination of Desolation occurs in the middle of the Tribulation (see Daniel 9:27), so these scholars believe that the Seal Judgments are earlier in that first half.

The next set of judgments after the Seal Judgments are the Trumpet Judgments (see Revelation 8:6 through chapter 11). They are generally more severe than the Seal Judgments. They are referred to by some as the "Judgment of Thirds," because in five of the Trumpet Judgments, the severe judgment is on one-third of something (or somethings). There is disagreement among scholars concerning the timing of the Trumpet Judgments. Some believe they will occur in the first half of the Tribulation, and others believe they will happen in the second half. While I could go either way, I lean toward the first half of the Tribulation. If you believe Revelation is chronological in order, the Trumpet Judgments are recorded by the apostle John before the mid-Tribulation events of Revelation chapters 11 through 13.

Chapter **14** talks again about the 144,000 Jews who serve Jesus and how they, along with the angels, are preaching the everlasting gospel. We also discover in this chapter that anyone who receives the Mark of the Beast will suffer eternal damnation because it is an unforgivable sin.

Chapters **15–16** are about the Bowl Judgments. These occur in the last three and a half years of the Tribulation, and they are horrific. These are the worst judgments of all time. Jesus said, "For then there will be **great tribulation**, such as has not been since the beginning of the world until this time, no, nor ever shall be" (Matthew 24:21, bold mine). The term "Great Tribulation" is coined by Jesus in that verse. It refers to the last half of the Tribulation where the Bowl Judgments of Revelation chapters 15 and 16 occur. These are the most horrific judgments of all, and they are universal in their effects.

Chapters **17–18** show us God's final judgment on the city and spirit of Babylon, which is both a religious and commercial entity that defies God's authority and seeks to replace Him in the hearts of men. The fate of Babylon goes all the way back to the book of Genesis, when man's first organized rebellion after the fall of Adam and Eve was led by Nimrod as he and his followers sought to "make a name for ourselves" (Genesis 11:4) and become their own gods. The spirit of Babylon has been in the world for thousands of years and is behind every act of rebellion against God. Finally, once and for all, it is judged and destroyed.

Chapter **19** contains the Marriage Supper of the Lamb as well as the Second Coming of Christ and the Church to the earth.

In chapter **20**, Satan is bound for 1,000 years, which coincides with the Millennial Rule of Christ and His saints. Chapter 20 ends with the Great White Throne Judgment, in which unbelievers from all times are sentenced to Hell.

Chapters **21–22** record the destruction of the current Heaven and Earth. A New Heaven and a New Earth are created, and New Jerusalem comes down from Heaven to the newly created Earth. This is where believers will spend eternity with God.

So yes, I believe Revelation is generally linear and chronological, and I hope the way I have presented this answer will help you understand that. I also hope it will make the book of Revelation easier for you to understand. It is the only book in the Bible that promises a special blessing to those who read it. Therefore, we need to take the mystery out of it and make it easier to understand.

> Blessed is the one who reads aloud the words of this prophecy, and blessed are those who hear it and take to heart what is written in it, because the time is near (Revelation 1:3 NIV).

9

Am I Really Saved?

I have asked Jesus to come into my heart and be Lord of my life probably over 500 times. I still don't have peace about my security. I've read and heard many pastors say God will turn away many people who "think" they're saved. How can I know I won't be turned away? How can I know whether I am saved or not?

—Shannon

This is a very common question pastors receive. In my book *Look Up!* I wrote about John Bunyan, the author of *Pilgrim's Progress.* Bunyan was a great man of faith, but even he went through a period of his life when he struggled to believe that God really wanted to save him. The truth is that if you are serious about following the Lord, then of course, you want to make sure you are doing it in the right way. However, I can tell you the only way to follow Jesus is to put your faith in what God says in His Word. Don't let your feelings become your compass; instead, make the Bible your guide.

In Romans 10:9–11, the apostle Paul says,

> If you confess with your mouth the Lord Jesus and believe in your heart that God has raised Him from the dead, you will be saved. For with the heart one believes unto righteousness, and with the mouth confession is made unto salvation. For the Scripture says, "Whoever believes on Him will not be put to shame."

If you are struggling with uncertainty about your own salvation, then I encourage you to say this prayer right now:

> *Jesus, You're my Lord, and I believe God raised You from the dead. I believe You are the only Savior of the world that God the Father has chosen and approved. I believe You are the Son of God, Your death*

26

paid for my sins, and through Your Resurrection You guaranteed my salvation. In Jesus' name, Amen.

If you will say these words to Christ Jesus and believe them, then the Bible says that you are saved.

Paul also says this in Ephesians:

> But God, who is rich in mercy, because of His great love with which He loved us, even when we were dead in trespasses, made us alive together with Christ (by grace you have been saved), and raised *us* up together, and made *us* sit together in the heavenly *places* in Christ Jesus, that in the ages to come He might show the exceeding riches of His grace in *His* kindness toward us in Christ Jesus. For by grace you have been saved through faith, and that not of yourselves; *it is* the gift of God, not of works, lest anyone should boast (2:4–9).

There were two thieves who were crucified next to Jesus. Probably neither one of them had ever done anything good in their lives. One of them mocked and rejected Jesus, but the other man had a very different reaction:

> Then he said to Jesus, "Lord, remember me when You come into Your kingdom." And Jesus said to him, "Assuredly, I say to you, today you will be with Me in Paradise" (Luke 23:42–43).

That's how easy it is to get to Heaven.

If you have come to Jesus 500 times because you are fearful for your salvation, then you're making it look really hard. It's not hard at all. Your salvation does not depend on you and your behavior, because it is by grace that we are saved. God loves you more than you can possibly comprehend. You don't need to say a prayer of salvation one more time. If you have confessed Jesus as your Lord and you believe God raised Him from the dead, then you are saved. Put your confidence in the love and grace of God, not in yourself. It's not about you or your efforts—it's about Jesus and what He has done. We don't get saved because of us. We get saved *in spite of us* because of our faith in Jesus.

10

Should I Be Re-Baptized?

What if you were baptized years ago as an adult when you first became a Christian but fell away for a time? Do you need to be re-baptized?

—Danielle

No, I do not believe you need to be baptized again, but with an important qualifier—*were you saved?* If you genuinely gave your heart to Christ and were baptized, then you were baptized according to what the Bible teaches.

In a way, it's kind of like saying you got married but then went through a really bad time in your relationship. Maybe someone cheated or did something else that was awful. Does that couple need to go through another wedding ceremony to be officially married? Of course they don't. They might need a lot of counseling and repentance. They may want to renew their vows as a symbol of their recommitment to the marriage, but there is no rule that says they must.

If you have fallen away from the Lord, then you just need to come back. Just turn your heart back to Him. Now, let me say if you feel convicted that you must be re-baptized as a sign of your repentance and returning to God, then there's nothing wrong with doing that. I certainly wouldn't tell anyone not to follow what they believe the Holy Spirit is leading them to do.

However, baptism is a very sacred thing, and when you're baptized, then you're baptized into Christ. When you are baptized into Christ, even though you may have wandered away, you can be sure Jesus didn't wander from you. You're still saved. You are still on your way to Heaven. Returning your heart is the big deal. I don't want to diminish that major movement in your life. But I don't believe you need to be re-baptized to be saved or to go in the Rapture with Jesus.

11

Do I Have to Go to Church?

When you say the Lord will come for His Church at the Rapture, what does that mean for those who do not have a "home" church, even though they love the Lord, study the Bible, and watch church online? Would they still be considered part of the Church when Jesus comes?
—Cheryl

Yes. Period. If you know Jesus as Lord and Savior, then, yes, you will go to Heaven! If this is something that you worry about, I want you to stop worrying. Your church attendance will not impact whether you are taken in the Rapture or whether you go to Heaven.

But I do want to say this: In the New Testament, Christians, by definition, met with other Christians. In fact, the first time the followers of Jesus were called Christians was because of their relationship with one another in the local church (see Acts 11:26). If someone says they are a Christian, but they have no desire to interact with other believers, they might be saved, but there's something unhealthy going on.

Here's what the writer of Hebrews says:

> And let us consider one another in order to stir up love and good works, not forsaking the assembling of ourselves together, as *is* the manner of some, but exhorting *one another*, and so much the more as you see the Day approaching (Hebrews 10:24–25).

First, it's going to be very difficult to "stir up" your fellow believers to love and good works if you have no relationship with them. Second, we need exhortation, which includes words of instruction and encouragement. How can we receive those if we don't have relationships with other Christians? Watching church online is obviously a means by which we can receive instruction and

29

encouragement, and it is the next best thing to being there in person. But it is difficult to give to others when we aren't with them in person.

The writer of Hebrews communicates how serious and urgent this matter really is by putting it in the context of "the Day approaching." That Day—with a capital D—is a reference to the return of Jesus.

I've been a pastor for more than 40 years, so I'm not going to give anyone an excuse to be absent from church. We need it. We need fellowship. We need uplifting relationships. All of us. I do realize there are people who are homebound and cannot physically attend church. I also realize there are people who live in remote communities where they don't have a church to attend. I think it is great that so many churches are offering online services for them to be able to enjoy. In fact, many churches now offer an "online campus" where pastors are connecting with people who can't be there physically. I think that is great, and it offers a sense of connection, care, and accountability for those who watch online. If you have to watch online, I would encourage you to be as connected as possible.

I also realize that during the COVID-19 epidemic, many people had to watch church services online because their church wasn't meeting in person. Sadly, during COVID, many people got in the habit of watching online and never went back to church when the epidemic was over. If you fall into that category, I would simply encourage you to make a commitment to physically go to church at least once a month. I realize that watching church online can be anointed and blessed, and I'm not diminishing that. But I am saying that something happens when we are around other believers that doesn't happen when we are alone.

If at all possible, it's healthy to avoid isolating ourselves at home. Being a Christian isn't simply a matter of how we can stay out of Hell. It's a matter of wisdom and living our lives here on earth in obedience to God and His will for our lives!

You are probably familiar with this verse:

> Be sober, be vigilant; because your adversary the devil walks about like a roaring lion, seeking whom he may devour (1 Peter 5:8).

But don't just read that single verse. I encourage you to read the verses that surround it. The apostle Peter is telling his readers that one of the ways to resist the devil is by submitting themselves to the local church.

You see, the devil is like a lion or a wolf that is always looking for the sheep farthest away from the shepherd and the rest of the flock. It picks up those straggling sheep on the margins—those who stray away from the group. Our ultimate strength is when we stay as close as possible to the Shepherd, who is Jesus. But we are also safer, spiritually speaking, when we stick close to a lot of other sheep! There is strength in numbers. Also, God has put gifts in you that others need. When you are alone, you are robbing others of the blessings you can offer them.

Did you realize the only group of people who did not suffer serious mental decline during the height of the COVID-19 pandemic were those who regularly attended church? If people did have mental health issues, then the church was one of the few places offering consistency and stability.

It is so important to be a part of a church. Skipping church won't keep you out of Heaven, but I know from 50 years of personal experience that life on earth is so much better when we spend it with other believers. You don't have to be a church nerd or a religious Pharisee about church attendance, but you do need to have a church home and be a part of a family of believers, large or small, if it is possible. It's not a matter of your eternal destination—just your temporal wellbeing and development.

12

Faith or Works?

Can you explain the meaning of "Faith without works is dead?" Do we have to do good works in order to be saved?
—**Kristen**

Good works do not save us, nor are they necessary for salvation. I understand how people can get this wrong impression from reading the book of James. James says,

> But someone will say, "You have faith, and I have works." Show me your faith without your works, and I will show you my faith by my works (2:18).

James gives this example:

> If a brother or sister is naked and destitute of daily food, and one of you says to them, "Depart in peace, be warmed and filled," but you do not give them the things which are needed for the body, what *does it* profit? (2:15–16)

Then he offers this conclusion:

> Thus also faith by itself, if it does not have works, is dead (2:17).

How, then, can we reconcile what James says with what Paul writes in Ephesians?

> For by grace you have been saved through faith, and that not of yourselves; *it is* the gift of God, not of works, lest anyone should boast (Ephesians 2:8–9).

No one gets saved by works. Works are not required for salvation. Paul tells the Ephesians that we are saved by grace, but in the very next verse he reminds them that God created us to do good works (v. 10). The works do not save us, but salvation makes us want to do them.

The only requirement to be saved is for us to accept Jesus Christ into our hearts. Salvation is an act of grace as we receive Jesus as the Lord of our lives and believe God has raised Him from the dead (see Romans 10:9–10). We recognize Jesus as our one and only hope of salvation. He is God's Son, and He is who He says He is.

How, then, should we think about works? What is James talking about? He is not talking about salvation. He's talking about how we live among other people. This is the social aspect of our relationship with Jesus and others. When Christians live among other people, and we see people in need, then we offer help as we are able. James is essentially saying if you don't want to help other people in need, then what good is your faith?

In a practical way, what is your life about if you have no desire to show the love of God to others? Jesus came to earth to save people. So as His followers, we would naturally want to help people. We can't save people, but our actions point them to the One who can. If you see somebody in need, then you're going to try to help that person.

What James is saying here is challenging but also very important. Believers are supposed to be the light of the world. Jesus said,

> You are the light of the world. A city that is set on a hill cannot be hidden. Nor do they light a lamp and put it under a basket, but on a lampstand, and it gives light to all *who are* in the house. Let your light so shine before men, that they may see your good works and glorify your Father in heaven (Matthew 5:14–16).

People judge Jesus by our actions. We might think they shouldn't, but they simply do. If we are uncaring, unhelpful, critical, condescending, or self-righteous, then they will try to say Jesus is that way too. They're not going to listen to our message. However, if we are compassionate, helpful, beneficial, merciful, and a source of strength in time of need, then people will find both Jesus and us attractive. Our actions may be just the thing that will open their hearts to the gospel.

I think what James is saying here is, "Be relationally responsible as a believer to do good in the name of Jesus for those people around you." Even so, you are not saved by works. You are absolutely saved by grace. It is the gift of God and God alone.

13

Will Sinners Be Raptured?

Concerning sin as a lifestyle, if someone is practicing fornication, adultery, or homosexuality, then will they be taken in the Rapture? Or will they still have time during the Tribulation to confess their sin and turn away from their lifestyle?

—Carol

Everyone who is alive during the Tribulation will have an opportunity to repent. If they have already died, then they will not. There are two keywords in this question: *lifestyle* and *practice*.

In 1 Corinthians chapter 6, Paul writes,

> Do you not know that the unrighteous will not inherit the kingdom of God? Do not be deceived. Neither fornicators, nor idolaters, nor adulterers, nor homosexuals, nor sodomites, nor thieves, nor covetous, nor drunkards, nor revilers, nor extortioners will inherit the kingdom of God. And such were some of you. But you were washed, but you were sanctified, but you were justified in the name of the Lord Jesus and by the Spirit of our God (vv. 9–11).

Pay close attention to what Paul says in these verses. He not only addresses sexual sin, but his list also includes people who covet, steal, and worship idols. Many Christians miss just how big this list really is. I am sure there are a lot of Christians who covet and drink to the point of drunkenness. A reviler is someone who speaks contemptuously to or about another person. In other words, they use mean words to hurt other people. Extortioners too will not inherit the Kingdom of God.

However, this is not a list of the worst people you can think of, like people on death row for a heinous murder. Paul is describing common people, including Christians, by labeling them with sins he knows they commonly practice. If they are paying attention, then they had better hear Paul's warning: *you are in danger!*

Paul is describing a lifestyle of sin. All of us commit sin, but there's a categorical difference between *committing sin* and *practicing it*. If I practice sin, then it means I'm not going to repent; rather, I'm going keep doing what I do, and that is just the way it's going to be. No one, including God, can tell me any different. When the Holy Spirit knocks on the door of my heart, I will pretend I don't hear Him. If He tries to come in, then I will double bolt the door.

In Galatians chapter 5, Paul says,

> Now the works of the flesh are evident, which are: adultery, fornication, uncleanness, lewdness, idolatry, sorcery, hatred, contentions, jealousies, outbursts of wrath, selfish ambitions, dissensions, heresies, envy, murders, drunkenness, revelries, and the like; of which I tell you beforehand, just as I also told *you* in time past, that those who practice such things will not inherit the kingdom of God (vv. 19–21).

All of these things Paul writes about describe people who are completely rebellious in their lifestyle. They are saying, "Jesus is not my Lord, and I have no intention of stopping what I'm doing. I'm not at all convicted by this whatsoever."

We are all sinners. No one is perfect. Sometimes I am asked if sinners will be raptured. If they aren't, then none of us are going. Everyone who goes in the Rapture will be a sinner. We will all be imperfect.

Nevertheless, there is a big difference between practicing sin, which means you have made it a lifestyle, and committing sin, which means you struggle but you keep returning to God with a repentant heart. All of us struggle to some degree. So if you're a person who makes mistakes and sins but still loves and serves Jesus, then you're going to go in the Rapture.

However, if you are a person who has a lifestyle of rebellion against God, then you should check your heart because there is something wrong with your relationship with Him. Understand that the Bible is not just talking about sex. It is also talking about lying, outbursts of anger, murder, envy, and all those kinds of things. If Jesus is the Lord of your life, then you're going to have some level of conviction when you sin. You will respond with repentance and faith. If that is not your response, then I would urge you to surrender to the Lordship of Jesus and ask God to change your heart and mind.

14

Can I Lose My Salvation?

Matthew 7:21–23 seems to indicate it's possible for people to lose their salvation? Can you explain these verses?

—Pam

Here are those verses, and this is Jesus speaking:

> Not everyone who says to Me, "Lord, Lord," shall enter the kingdom of heaven, but he who does the will of My Father in heaven. Many will say to Me in that day, "Lord, Lord, have we not prophesied in Your name, cast out demons in Your name, and done many wonders in Your name?" And then I will declare to them, "I never knew you; depart from Me, you who practice lawlessness!"

As a longtime pastor, I can tell you this question (or something similar to it) is common. But I will deal specifically with this passage.

In these verses Jesus says, "I **never** knew you" (bold mine). So the people He is speaking about didn't lose their salvation—*they never had it.* These are people who like to carry the title "Christian" and do Christian stuff, but they have no relationship with Jesus Christ. They've never had one. The worst part of this situation is that some other unbelievers look at them and assume those are Christians when they really aren't. These people couldn't lose their salvation because they haven't been saved. Christianity is not a religion; it's a relationship. If there's no relationship with Jesus, then there's no salvation.

I want to make a very important yet simple statement: **The family of God is the most secure family in the world.** If you have come to Jesus with repentance and faith and given yourself to Him, then you don't have to worry about losing your salvation—ever.

I know some people lose things like their car keys all the time. It's like they practice at least once a week for the annual Easter egg hunt by doing a hunt for keys. But salvation isn't the same as car keys—you don't have to hunt for your salvation all the time. When you do something wrong, you don't have to get saved all over again. That kind of thinking is nonsense. If you're saved, then you're saved.

That brings me to another important part of this issue. We are living in a day that is both momentous and evil at the same time. Many people who claimed to be Christians, including some pastors, are publicly renouncing their faith in Jesus Christ. They're simply saying, "I'm not a Christian anymore." It's a shocking situation, but it's not a new one. Some people were doing that all the way back in the New Testament days.

The writer of Hebrews says this about people who renounce the faith:

> For *it is* impossible for those who were once enlightened, and have tasted the heavenly gift, and have become partakers of the Holy Spirit, and have tasted the good word of God and the powers of the age to come, if they fall away, to renew them again to repentance, since they crucify again for themselves the Son of God, and put *Him* to an open shame.
>
> For the earth which drinks in the rain that often comes upon it, and bears herbs useful for those by whom it is cultivated, receives blessing from God; but if it bears thorns and briers, *it is* rejected and near to being cursed, whose end *is* to be burned (6:4–8).

So you can see people renouncing the faith isn't something new. I had a friend who was a worship leader, and I was pretty close to him and his wife for several years. I went to speak at the church where he had been leading worship and discovered he has 100 percent renounced Jesus Christ. This man wasn't an average churchgoer; he was an established worship leader! I believe he was saved. I really do. Then he completely renounced Jesus.

I have to ask, *What about people like that?* According to Hebrews chapter 6, when a person has experienced the rain, tasted of the heavenly gift and the good things of the age to come, and then renounced it … well, *they can't repent.* A person who does that has crucified Jesus all over again.

That leads me to a final issue. I didn't lose my free will when I got saved, and salvation is not a prison. What happens when a person is saved and has experienced Jesus, but then wakes up one day and says, "Nah, I've decided don't want this anymore. Everything I once believed, I now reject"? What I mean is they have completely renounced Jesus Christ. Does that mean they have lost their salvation? No, it does not; *they forfeited it.* As I said, the Christian family is the most secure family on earth. That means we can sin and make mistakes, but we're still saved. You can't lose your salvation, but is it possible to renounce it and give it back? Hebrews seems to say it is, and *I sure wouldn't try it.* Because once someone sincerely renounces Jesus, they are in grave danger.

This doesn't mean you got angry at God over something and told Him you hated Him. I have known many people who went through tough times and got mad at God and later repented. Renouncing your faith is a cold, calculated action. It is basically renouncing Christ and your decision to follow Him. It is announcing to the world that your faith in Him was a mistake, and you are a disappointed customer. That is why it is such a serious issue! According to the writer of Hebrews, those who do this "crucify again for themselves the Son of God, and put Him to an open shame."

15

Who Will Be Raptured?

**What qualifies or disqualifies someone from the Rapture?
Some people believe that once we accept Jesus, we have
salvation, and nothing can keep us from Heaven unless
we reject Him completely. Others say that unless we completely stop sinning and stay in communication with Jesus,
He will say He never really knew us. Which view is correct?
What happens if someone is sinning when the Rapture
happens?**

—Carol

Let's look at a few passages of Scripture that are relevant to your
question. You are probably familiar with John 3:16:

For God so loved the world that He gave His only begotten Son,
that whoever believes in Him should not perish but have everlasting
life.

Then in Romans 10:9, Paul says,

If you confess with your mouth the Lord Jesus and believe in your
heart that God has raised Him from the dead, you will be saved.

Also, remember this scene with Jesus on the cross and the two
thieves on either side of Him:

Then one of the criminals who were hanged blasphemed Him, saying,
"If You are the Christ, save Yourself and us."

But the other, answering, rebuked him, saying, "Do you not even
fear God, seeing you are under the same condemnation? And we
indeed justly, for we receive the due reward of our deeds; but this Man
has done nothing wrong." Then he said to Jesus, "Lord, remember me
when You come into Your kingdom."

And Jesus said to him, "Assuredly, I say to you, today you will be
with Me in Paradise" (Luke 23:39–43).

40

The second thief's confession is what released the salvation he received. We need both confession and belief.

Finally, consider 2 Corinthians 5:17, which says,

> Therefore, if anyone *is* in Christ, *he is* a new creation; old things have passed away; behold, all things have become new.

I think both views have some validity. First, we are saved by grace through faith. There's nothing we can do to earn our own salvation. We are not perfect. I do not believe any of us can completely stop sinning this side of Heaven. People are just going to sin. However, we can and should do our very best to stop and repent, especially regarding certain types of sin that involve other people. The Bible says our righteousness is like filthy rags (see Isaiah 64:6). There's never a day in my life when I will merit God's love or grace. Salvation is always a gift God gives to us.

The second point of view also has some correct assumptions. Saved people need to be different. What I mean is that if we are saved, then something needs to change in our lives. If someone says they are a Christian but they live like an unbeliever, then nothing has really changed. If that is the case, they need to ask themselves some serious questions, and they particularly need to ask God to reveal their spiritual situation. If the old has passed away, then the new must come. Saved people will act like saved people.

I do believe that if you, as a true believer, are actively involved in a very serious sin when Jesus comes, then you will have to deal with Him over that in some way. Paul tells us that some people have lives built on the foundation of wood, hay, and straw. Others stand on gold, silver, and precious stones (see 1 Corinthians 3:9–15). In other words, our works are related to our eternal condition. If all we do is live for the world and for ourselves, then that is wood, hay, and straw. Paul says we still get to Heaven, "yet so as through fire" (v. 15). The things we do in this world that are wrong, sinful, and selfish are only temporal. They will not last; they are not eternal. Those things will be burned up when we stand in judgment before Jesus. So if a true believer is sinning when the Rapture occurs, it doesn't mean they will be left behind, but it does mean God will deal with them about it.

The Judgment Seat of Christ will happen at the Rapture. It's a judgment of rewards, and everyone in that judgment will go to Heaven. However, there will be scrutiny (not punishment) at that judgment. The things in our lives that are wrong and sinful and that separate us from God (wood, hay, and straw) will be consumed and forever lost. The good things we have done in our lives (gold, silver, and precious stones) will be rewarded and will stay with us for all eternity. We must remember that we are saved by grace, but we are judged by our works. Jesus said,

> And behold, I am coming quickly, and My reward *is* with Me, to give to every one according to his work (Revelation 22:12).

So I want to come back and summarize my answer:

- We are saved by grace, not by works.
- Saved people have changed lives.
- Saved people will go with Jesus in the Rapture.
- Saved people will go to Heaven.
- If we, as true believers, engage in serious sin, then God will deal with us at the time of the Rapture at the Judgment Seat of Christ, but we are still saved and will go to Heaven.

At 19 years old, I was a professional heathen. I wasn't an amateur; I had turned pro. But when I got saved, everything began to change in my life. I was still imperfect and needed to go through a redemption process. In fact, God is still taking me through that process, but my life started changing immediately when I got saved. People who knew me before I was a Christian recognized things had changed. God wants to change us. If we are believers, He will ultimately change us into the likeness of Jesus.

16

Will My Habit Keep Me from the Rapture?

I am trying to stop vaping. I've thrown everything away, but then I picked it back up again. I'm worried my disobedience will keep me from the Rapture.

—Bonnie

First, I understand what you are experiencing. I went through something like this myself. I started smoking when I was 15, and I did not quit until I was 25. It was one of the hardest things I've ever done. I enjoyed smoking. I really did. But the Lord spoke to me and told me He wasn't going to use me in the way He wanted if I kept smoking. He had called me to preach when I got saved at 19 years old.

Of course, the Lord doesn't want us to hurt our bodies. The apostle Paul reminds us that our bodies are the temple of the Holy Spirit (see 1 Corinthians 6:19). Smoking is bad for our bodies, but I was once very addicted to it. Mark Twain is known to have said, "Giving up smoking is the easiest thing in the world. I know because I've done it thousands of times." I don't know if Mark Twain ever stopped smoking, but I do know he wrote several times about what a struggle it is to quit. I can relate to that. I tried to quit a hundred times, but it was the Holy Spirit who helped me succeed.

One morning, I was smoking while having a quiet time and praying. The Lord spoke to me and said, "Say that you're a nonsmoker." He literally said that to me. "From now on, just say you're a nonsmoker." That is how I stopped smoking. It was a supernatural thing. I had tried to stop many times before that day, but I couldn't do it on my own.

The only thing that qualifies you for the Rapture is knowing Jesus Christ as your Lord and Savior. If you are a Christian, then you're going in the Rapture. You could be vaping at that very moment. There will be many Christians who will be doing bad things when the Rapture happens, but they are still going to go. Thank God we are saved by grace and not by works.

People ask many "What if" questions about the Rapture—"What if I'm _____ (naked, having sex, going to the bathroom, etc.) when Jesus comes?" You can fill in the blank with your own question. But it doesn't matter where you are because the Rapture will happen in a "moment." The Greek word that is translated "moment" is *atomos*. This is where we get the word *atom*. It is an indivisible amount of time. Listen to what Jesus said:

> When He had called the multitude to *Himself*, He said to them, "Hear and understand: Not what goes into the mouth defiles a man; but what comes out of the mouth, this defiles a man" (Matthew 15:10–11).

The Jewish religious leaders of Jesus' day declared all sorts of eating, drinking, and other customs as "sin." They made things sin that are not even in the Bible. Jesus said what is going to corrupt us in terms of eternity is what comes out of us, not what goes into us.

By the way, there are actually only two unforgivable sins in the Bible:

- To call the Holy Spirit evil or blaspheme against Him (Matthew 12:31–32)
- To take the Mark of the Beast (Revelation 14:9–11).

In other words, two sins will keep people out of Heaven, but vaping is not one of them. Now, I would strongly encourage you not to vape. Medical researchers are finding out more every day about how it hurts our bodies. Do everything you can to stop. Pray and ask the Holy Spirit to help you because you know it is not good for you. But understand that it is not an eternal issue. You are not going to go to Hell because you vape, but you might get to Heaven quicker if you compromise your health!

17

How Can I Be a Good Steward?

I'm wondering about stewardship and the Rapture. We have been blessed with many responsibilities and have been charged to be good stewards of those things while we are here on earth. What about post-Rapture? I find myself stocking my pantry and strategically placing Bibles for people who are left behind, but I'm also wondering how I can continue to take care of my animals, people I support at my job, and other things once I'm gone.

—Laura

It's really great that you would think about those types of things. It shows you are incredibly compassionate and responsible. I commend you for it.

In Matthew chapter 25, Jesus tells two parables and one true story about the judgments that will happen when He returns. The first parable is about the wise and foolish virgins. The second is about a man who goes on a trip and leaves his property under the charge of three servants. It is a parable about *stewardship*. At the end of that second parable, the owner asks his three servants to give an account of what they have done with his property.

After the Rapture, stewardship as we know it will completely disappear. We will be rewarded for our obedience on earth and enter into our eternal relationship with Jesus. We won't worry about the choices we made because we will be in eternity with Him. God will reward us for whatever good we've done and whatever we have stewarded well in this life. But you are asking, "How can I take care of the people I'm taking care of now at work or wherever they might be? How can I provide for my pets?" I think you need to do your best while you are still here and trust God when you are gone. He cares about those we love even more than we do! You can trust Him!

At our prophecy conference last year, we had a panel of our speakers. One person asked, "Are pets going to go to Heaven?" The panel's resounding answer was, "Yes, they are going to go to Heaven." Many Bible scholars agree with that answer. But I think that you just have to trust that the Lord is going to take care of everything after the Rapture. Really, I believe that's the only thing we can do.

18

What Happens to Pets?

What will happen to our beloved pets after the Rapture? Should we prepare? We are very concerned.
—Mary & Rachel

I commend you for your love for your pets. I know a lot of people who feel the same way. God loves us as a Father, so He is also very caring for us and our animals.

I can't speak with authority about something the Bible doesn't talk much about, but I can speak with authority about the nature of God. God is a loving God, and He loves us, our families, and our pets. So I would encourage you to pray about it and let the Lord direct you as you make arrangements for your pets. I know there are some insurance programs and kennels who will take in pets if someone dies, so I think you could set up a similar situation in case of the Rapture (assuming not everyone with the program is a believer). I don't know the details of all those programs, but I would recommend doing some research.

The Bible tells us that righteous people care for their animals. So if you're a righteous person, you will care for your pets. I can tell you this one thing: You're not going to be worried after the Rapture. When you're in Heaven at the Marriage Supper of the Lamb, you're not going to be concerned about one single thing here on the earth. You won't wonder whether you left the iron on or the water running. I just think it is the nature of God to care about animals. I can promise God loves you and cares about the things you care about, and I would just make it a matter of prayer. Trust that God loves your pets and that He will care for them after you are raptured.

19

Should I Watch the News?

I want to stay somewhat current on world events, but I stopped watching the news two years ago because my wife and I found ourselves becoming constantly angry. What is the right balance between being informed about factual current events and going overboard and falling into the devil's traps of anxiety and worry?

—Scott

I definitely can relate to this question. One day, as I was studying in my office, I had the TV turned on to a cable news channel, and it was just playing in the background all day long. The volume was turned off, but I could see the video images, many of which were repeated throughout the day.

I found myself becoming increasingly troubled, especially as the day went on. Why? It wasn't anything in particular. It was just that, in real time, I was paying attention to the worst things happening in the world all day long.

Watching the news can influence your mindset. I'm reminded of Paul's instructions in Philippians chapter 4 about what should fill our minds:

> Finally, brethren, whatever things are true, whatever things *are* noble, whatever things *are* just, whatever things *are* pure, whatever things *are* lovely, whatever things *are* of good report, *if there* is any virtue and *if there* is anything praiseworthy—meditate on these things (v. 8).

If we keep the news on 24/7, regardless of what station we are watching, then it's doubtful that we are meditating on things that are "lovely" or "pure" or "of good report." It's more likely we are filling our minds with things that make us anxious.

With that said, I do watch some local and national television news and read news items when I am writing articles for *Tipping Point*. In that case, I am not mindlessly scrolling through news sites but watching with purpose. I am looking up specific End Times information for research, rather than for entertainment. This type of news doesn't bother me because of my understanding of the End Times. It actually helps me focus more on what the Bible says.

However, if I just sit and watch the news all day or keep scrolling through headlines on my smartphone or laptop, then I'm definitely going to experience increasing anxiety. Regarding news on television, I have become very careful about how much I watch. My television viewing is mostly limited to the weather, sports, and maybe 30 minutes of news each day beyond what I find on the internet.

Some homes or offices just have news programs running all day long, but I think it's healthier to limit your time and exposure to the news. When your spirit starts getting upset, that's when you know it's time to turn it off.

I recommend balancing all the information you receive with prayer. When you see something upsetting, don't just internalize it, swallow it down, and let it stew in anxiety and worry. Externalize it, which means pray about it.

> Be anxious for nothing, but in everything by prayer and supplication, with thanksgiving, let your requests be made known to God; and the peace of God, which surpasses all understanding, will guard your hearts and minds through Christ Jesus (Philippians 4:6–7).

In response to this question, I would say that it is good to catch up with the news every day to the degree that it is informative and not upsetting. I like knowing what is going on around me, but I will not allow it to oppress me and rob me of my peace. I believe when the news makes us angry, it is because we are being focused on fallen man and losing our focus on God. That is why we must prioritize the Word of God and prayer over being exposed to endless news cycles that cause anger and anxiety to grow within us.

20

Should I Obey Every Law?

If we believe that the time of the Rapture is very near, then should we bother fighting some of the government mandates that we see these days? If things are going to just get worse and there's no stopping it, then should we just be focused on "making disciples" instead of pushing back against ungodly laws and mandates?

—Gordon

This is an important question and brings up a very concerning situation. Should we try to redeem America or the country where we reside? Or should we spend our remaining time trying to win people to Christ? I think the correct answer is that we should do both.

First, we need to consider what Paul wrote in his letter to the Romans:

> Let everyone be subject to the governing authorities, for there is no authority except that which God has established. The authorities that exist have been established by God. Consequently, whoever rebels against the authority is rebelling against what God has instituted, and those who do so will bring judgment on themselves (13:1–2 NIV).

Paul wrote these words when the evil Roman emperor Nero was in power. Nero persecuted Christians! But Paul said that Christians are to honor and obey their ruling authorities because, in some way, God has elevated them to that position of power. As Daniel 2:21 puts it, "He removes kings and raises up kings."

Now, this doesn't mean God approves of everything that happens at the governmental level. Far from it! When the laws of man are in direct conflict with the laws of God, then I believe it is necessary for Christians to push back. We see examples of this all throughout Scripture, including in the book of Acts when the Sanhedrin forbade Peter and John from teaching about the Resurrection of Jesus. The apostles refused to be quiet because following the laws of their authorities would have meant breaking God's law.

As citizens of the United States, we will lose our freedoms if we don't stand up for them. We've seen many recent events that demonstrate governmental tyranny. During the COVID-19 epidemic lockdown, there were some parts of the country where believers were forbidden to even gather or meet for worship. Was that an authoritative ruling we should obey or one we should push against?

Many churches fought back because the most sacred liberty we have is the freedom of religion—the freedom to practice our faith. This precious freedom is constantly under assault, and we have to fight to retain it.

The second liberty under assault is the freedom of speech—to be able to speak up and say the things we believe in without being censored or persecuted. It might be tempting for Christians to just pull away from the world altogether. That concerns me, though. If we just stay within the four walls of the church and don't involve ourselves in the community or the cause of our government, then there will be no one left to protect our freedoms, and we will lose them.

The worst-case scenario is that we begin to feel as if we are living in one of those countries around the world that our State Department is constantly warning us about. In some of those nations, religion and Christianity are outlawed and persecuted. If this ever becomes the case in the US, then we will have an entirely different set of problems.

I believe our responsibility is to focus both on making disciples and on standing up for what is right as citizens. Both choices are part of our Christian witness. We should be citizens of the Kingdom of God first, but we are also called to be good citizens of the countries in which we live.

21

Is Dispensationalism a New Teaching?

Some people say dispensationalism is a "new" teaching or only about 200 years old. If it is a view based on Scripture, then how can they claim that it's new?

—Suzanne

First, a few definitions. In the world of theology, the study of the End Times is known as *eschatology*. It has been part of Christianity since the earliest days of the Church. Dispensationalism is a systematic approach to understanding eschatology, and it was first laid out by an English Bible teacher named John Nelson Darby (1800–1882).

Other prominent American Bible scholars and theologians, including Cyrus Ingerson Scofield (1843–1921) and Dwight L. Moody (1837–1899), made further developments to dispensationalism and helped popularize this framework during their careers. Scofield wrote notes on dispensationalism for a Bible that is still popular today (*Scofield Reference Bible*), and Moody Bible Institute in Chicago became well-known because of its focus on dispensational theology. Because of this influence, many American Christians began reading the Bible with a fresh perspective—especially the End Times passages.

According to those early teachers of dispensationalism and their understanding of Scripture, humanity has and will experience different epochs or periods of history. They referred to these as "dispensations." God used these dispensations as teaching devices to help people understand His overall design and plan for humanity.

Depending on the teacher, the list of dispensations ranges from 7 to 15 epochs, depending on how that individual teacher identifies time periods. While there may be some variance, here are the core dispensations that scholars have listed over the years:

- **Innocence** (the time before the fall of Adam and Eve)
- **Conscience** (the time after the fall but before the Flood)
- **Human Governance** (the period after the Flood in which God allowed human government to maintain order)
- **Promise** (God's call to Abraham and the establishment of a covenant with His people)
- **Law** (the period after God gave the Law to Moses on Mount Sinai)
- **Grace** (the time beginning after the death and Resurrection of Jesus, through which God extends salvation to believers in Christ)
- **Kingdom Age** (the future reign of Jesus on earth for a thousand years and the establishment of His eternal Kingdom of righteousness).

Again, this list is by no means definitive. Bible teachers interpret God's Word in different ways, and some make their own adjustments, splitting some dispensations (like the Law period) into multiple parts. But the basic teachings of Dispensationalism remain the same. One of the noteworthy elements is that it distinguishes clearly between Israel and the Church. For instance, Old and New Testament prophecies about the nation of Israel are interpreted as being about Israel, separate from today's Church. (The Church includes all those who have been saved during the present "Grace" dispensation.)

You are probably wondering what I think about this. Yes, I refer to myself as a Dispensationalist. Despite some of the varying ways Dispensationalists understand the Bible, Dispensationalists, as a rule, believe in the Rapture and in taking prophecies about Israel literally.

Some people who don't like Rapture teaching or think it is over-emphasized will say, "Teaching about the Rapture didn't start until 200 years ago under John Nelson Darby." That's an easy way to set aside something that may make them uncomfortable or to dismiss pastors and theologians they disagree with.

But it's not so easy to dismiss the Rapture. If you dismiss the Rapture, then you will need to dismiss parts of the New Testament. You will need to throw out things Jesus said and things the apostle Paul taught, such as:

> But I do not want you to be ignorant, brethren, concerning those who have fallen asleep, lest you sorrow as others who have no hope. For if we believe that Jesus died and rose again, even so God will bring with Him those who sleep in Jesus.
>
> For this we say to you by the word of the Lord, that we who are alive *and* remain until the coming of the Lord will by no means precede those who are asleep. For the Lord Himself will descend from heaven with a shout, with the voice of an archangel, and with the trumpet of God. And the dead in Christ will rise first. Then we who are alive *and* remain shall be **caught up** together with them in the clouds to meet the Lord in the air. And thus we shall always be with the Lord. Therefore comfort one another with these words (1 Thessalonians 4:13–18, bold mine).

The English words "caught up" are from the Greek word *harpazo.* It means 'seize hastily.' When the Bible was translated into Latin, the word *rapturo* was used, and that is where we get our English word rapture. It is a biblical word and a very biblical truth.

As a whole, Dispensationalism may be relatively new in that it is a systematic way of teaching about the End Times. *But* teaching about the Rapture is not new. It has been taught since the first century, and teaching about it now is more important than ever.

So be careful when you hear people dismiss the Rapture because of John Nelson Darby or other Bible teachers who began talking about it frequently in the 1800s. I believe God had the Rapture in mind from the very beginning of time. Dispensational theology, as we understand it, may have been given a name and clarified in the 19th century, but scholars were interpreting the Bible literally and teaching about the End Times since the first century when the Church was born.

22

What About People with Other Views?

Should we leave Christians alone who have other views about the End Times? For example, should we let other people draw their own conclusions, such as preterists, people who hold to a post-Tribulation view of the Rapture, or those who believe in a "Kingdom Now" theology? Or should we try to lead them into the truth of what the Bible says? If they are saved, God is going to rapture them regardless, right? So should we bother with trying to correct them?

—Susan

Let me define some of the things you include in your question:

- **Preterists** believe End Times prophecies were fulfilled mostly in the first century AD with a few of them fulfilled as late as the fourth century AD. They believe nothing we read in the Bible today is an End Times prophecy, nor does anything relate to our current generation. Everything has already happened.
- **Post-Tribulation Proponents** believe the Rapture will occur at the end of the Tribulation.
- **Kingdom Now/Post-Millennial Supporters** believe God will reestablish control of the world through the Church before the return of Jesus at the end of the Millennium.

I have simplified those three views for the sake of brevity, but I do not misrepresent the major thrust of those belief systems. There are also a variety of other approaches to the End Times. It doesn't matter to me personally, and it certainly doesn't hurt my feelings if someone does not agree with me. However, if someone doesn't believe in Jesus, then that matters a great deal to me. I would say the same thing about a belief in Jesus' virgin birth and His blood atonement. Those matter to me; they are essentials to the faith that I deeply care about. I will be kind to everyone, but I won't be in close fellowship with someone who does not hold to essential Christian doctrines.

Nevertheless, what a person believes about the End Times doesn't matter to me, at least in terms of whether I will fellowship with them. I trust that *Jesus will be right on time*! It's all going to happen exactly the way the Bible says it will. I don't teach on the End Times to make anyone else look bad. I don't preach about the End Times as a way to argue someone else into accepting my position. I preach and teach on the End Times because it comforts people and helps believers prepare for what is coming.

When we understand what the Bible says about the End Times, it's comforting. It helps people contextualize what is happening in the world right now. It helps them to understand that the next major event that is going to happen is the Rapture of the Church. Believers are going to be spared the wrath of the Tribulation events. I know a lot of smart people who believe differently than me. So what do I do? *Nothing*. I don't try to argue with them. I just state what I believe the Bible is saying in a way that is clear and positive.

If someone is a believer, then they are going to go in the Rapture despite their beliefs about the End Times. Jesus is coming in the Rapture for all true believers. Some of them might be really surprised, but they're going anyway. Now, if someone does not believe in Jesus, then they're in serious trouble. But if you believe in Jesus and have different views on the End Times, then I don't think it matters as far as where you will spend eternity.

However, let me tell you where there is a problem with having an erroneous belief system about the End Times. Some teachers are upsetting other believers unnecessarily. Teachers who are telling believers that they will suffer through the Tribulation are very upsetting. I know there are some End Times teachers right now who are teaching on the End Times while selling survival gear at a healthy profit. I really despise that practice because it is profiteering off people's fears. I do have a few things around my house in case of a power outage, a flood, or something like that, but I am not a prepper in that way for the End Times. I say that because Jesus is coming, and believers are not going to go through the wrath that is to come.

> For they themselves declare concerning us what manner of entry we had to you, and how you turned to God from idols to serve the living and true God, and to wait for His Son from heaven, whom He raised from the dead, *even* **Jesus who delivers us from the wrath to come** (1 Thessalonians 1:9–10, bold mine).

23

Will Some Christians Not Be Raptured?

Is it true that when the Rapture takes place only half of the Christians will go while the other half remains? Would that be because some Christians are like the five virgins with oil while the other five are without oil (Matthew 25:1–13)? What are the characteristics of those who will go and those who will remain?

—Jean

The reason why some will go and others will remain is because of a personal relationship with Jesus Christ or a lack thereof. I believe the five virgins who go with the bridegroom represent those who have a personal relationship with Jesus. The five who are not taken represent those who say they are Christians but really are not.

Recently, I was in a conversation with someone, and I asked if they were a believer.

> "Yes," they replied.
> "That's great. When did you received Christ?"
> They responded, "Well, I was baptized as a child."
> I said, "Well, that doesn't count. Your parents can't make that decision for you. It's wonderful that your parents wanted to bring you into the church as a child, but you have to make a personal decision about your own faith in Christ."

At that point, the person became indignant. I thought they might say, "Oh, well, I didn't know that" but they didn't. Instead, they said, "No, no, I became a Christian as a child. I'm a Christian. So I'm going to Heaven or whatever."

There are three important truths we can learn from my conversation with that person:

1. CHRISTIANITY IS NOT A RELIGION.

I say Christianity isn't a religion in the sense that you simply join it, and that is all you need to do to get right with God. Rather, Christianity is a personal relationship with Jesus Christ. Do you know Jesus? Do you hear His voice? In the Gospel of John, Jesus says, "My sheep hear My voice, and I know them, and they follow Me" (10:27). So to be an authentic believer in Christ, you must have an active, personal relationship with Him.

2. CHRISTIANS ARE KNOWN BY THEIR LOVE AND THEIR FRUIT.

Christians are known by love and by the fruit of the Spirit in their lives. In the book of Matthew, Jesus said,

> Beware of false prophets, who come to you in sheep's clothing, but inwardly they are ravenous wolves. You will know them by their fruits. Do men gather grapes from thornbushes or figs from thistles? Even so, every good tree bears good fruit, but a bad tree bears bad fruit. A good tree cannot bear bad fruit, nor *can* a bad tree bear good fruit. Every tree that does not bear good fruit is cut down and thrown into the fire. Therefore by their fruits you will know them (7:15–20).

What is the fruit of the Spirit? In Galatians 5:22–23, Paul lists everything that makes up that fruit:

> But the fruit of the Spirit is love, joy, peace, longsuffering, kindness, goodness, faithfulness, gentleness, self-control. Against such there is no law.

No one is perfect, including believers. All of us have our moments when we fall short of God's expectations. However, we should have the fruit of a person who knows Jesus. He said we would know false prophets by their fruits, but believers are known by our fruits too. Figs don't grow on thistle trees. Figs are sweet, while thistles are prickly. Grapes don't come from thorn bushes. Again, one is sweet, while the other has thorns.

Ask yourself this question: *Is my personality kind, sweet, and good-natured, or am I mean, cantankerous, and angry?* If you realize you're often mean and angry, then you should check your fruit, because mean people are not showing they have the fruit of the Spirit, and if there is no fruit, then you might not actually know Jesus.

3. CHRISTIANS ARE PEOPLE OF THE WORD.

Do you believe God's Word, or are you always questioning it? Do you have faith in what God has said, or are you cynical and compromising? Christians believe the Bible and do everything they can to listen to the Holy Spirit and live by the principles of Scripture. The significance of the lamps in the parable of the Ten Virgins is that those lights represent the Word of God. When you walk in the light of His Word, that means you have a real relationship with the Lord. If you have no interest in obeying God and His Word, then something is way off. If so, you're walking in darkness and not in the Word. Again, none of us are without faults, but a personal relationship with Jesus is essential. You need Jesus to forgive you and cover you with the power of His shed blood. You can't get that forgiveness simply by being a good person or thinking you became a Christian because your parents told you that you are. It has to be your choice. Jesus made it possible for you to go to Heaven, but it is through a personal relationship with Him only.

24

Will There Be an End Times Revival?

I heard a couple of pastors talk about how there is going to be revival in the End Times. I don't see anything about a revival in Revelation. What do you think?

—Pamela

Many people are coming to Christ all around the world. I am excited to hear stories about China and the Middle East (especially Iran). I hear other reports from Africa, South America, and other areas where the Church is growing, and significant evangelism is taking place. Incredible numbers of people have been coming to Christ worldwide, but there is no huge pocket yet in America. Recently, a very significant move of the Holy Spirit occurred at Asbury University in Kentucky. It has encouraged many Christians, and I have written about that revival on endtimes.com. Time will tell if that movement spreads to signify mass evangelism.

In answering this question, let me distinguish between pre-Tribulation evangelism and post-Tribulation evangelism. I don't see any promise of mass revival occurring pre-Tribulation, even though I pray it does. In fact, in Luke chapter 17, Jesus draws a parallel between the time of the Rapture of the Church and the days of Noah and Lot just before they were removed and catastrophic judgment occurred. Jesus said His coming will be just like those days.

The days of Noah and Lot were times of unparalleled immorality and violence on earth. There was a righteous remnant living for God, but the rest of the world was corrupt and unrepentant. Interestingly, neither Noah nor Lot had one convert who was saved because of them.

In fact, Noah only took his seven family members onto the ark, and Lot actually lost his wife in the process of fleeing for his life. Only he and his two daughters made it out.

So not only do I not find a promise of worldwide revival before the Rapture, I also find Jesus' own words promising a world of godless rebellion with a righteous remnant living for Him—like Noah and Lot. In 2 Thessalonians chapter 2, the apostle Paul promises the same thing. He writes that just before the Rapture there will be a great apostasy (falling away from truth) that will signal the return of Jesus and the arrival of the Antichrist.

Having said all this, I'm very thankful that there are millions of people still being saved every year around the world, and I pray it will become a great revival and harvest before Jesus returns. However, I can't point to that promise in Scripture.

But there is a huge revival coming! It will be a post-Tribulation event occurring *after* the Rapture and during the Tribulation. Here is the record of it in Revelation chapter 7:

> After these things I looked, and behold, a great multitude which no one could number, of all nations, tribes, peoples, and tongues, standing before the throne and before the Lamb, clothed with white robes, with palm branches in their hands, and crying out with a loud voice, saying, "Salvation *belongs* to our God who sits on the throne, and to the Lamb!" All the angels stood around the throne and the elders and the four living creatures, and fell on their faces before the throne and worshiped God, saying:
> "Amen! Blessing and glory and wisdom,
> Thanksgiving and honor and power and might,
> *Be* to our God forever and ever.
> Amen."
> Then one of the elders answered, saying to me, "Who are these arrayed in white robes, and where did they come from?"
> And I said to him, "Sir, you know."
> So he said to me, "**These are the ones who come out of the great tribulation**, and washed their robes and made them white in the blood of the Lamb. Therefore they are before the throne of God, and serve Him day and night in His temple. And He who sits on the throne will dwell among them. They shall neither hunger anymore nor thirst anymore; the sun shall not strike them, nor any heat; for the Lamb who is in the midst of the throne will shepherd them and lead them

to living fountains of waters. And God will wipe away every tear from their eyes" (vv. 9–17, bold mine).

In Revelation chapter 14, we see the everlasting gospel being preached by the 144,000 Jewish witnesses and supernaturally by angels to every nation, tongue, and tribe on earth. The Tribulation will be a hellish time on the earth beyond anything we can comprehend. But for those left behind, it is God's time of final mercy for them to repent and come to Christ. Thankfully, "a great multitude which no one could number" will come to Him!

That is the only worldwide End Times revival I see promised in Scripture.

25

Will Everyone Hear the Gospel?

Does every ear have to hear the story of the gospel of Jesus Christ before the Rapture can take place? Someone told me there are still around 200–250 people groups in the world that have yet to be reached with the gospel, and until that takes place, Jesus cannot return. What are your thoughts on this?

—Kimberly

I do agree that the gospel will ultimately be preached to every people group. However, I don't agree that it is necessary for the Rapture to occur. The gospel definitely will be delivered to everyone by the end of the Tribulation, but maybe not before. I do hope the Church will preach the gospel everywhere. I hope it will happen before the Rapture, but it's not necessary for the Rapture to happen.

In fact, the gospel is going around the world right now via satellite radio, the internet, other types of electronic and digital delivery, and through human missionaries. Every tribe, tongue, and nation will have a chance to receive it before Jesus returns at the Second Coming.

Let me explain my reasoning for what I believe. I will start with Matthew's Gospel:

> Then they will deliver you up to tribulation and kill you, and you will be hated by all nations for My name's sake. And then many will be offended, will betray one another, and will hate one another. Then many false prophets will rise up and deceive many. And because lawlessness will abound, the love of many will grow cold. But he who endures to the end shall be saved. And this gospel of the kingdom will be preached in all the world as a witness to all the nations, and then the end will come.

Therefore when you see the "abomination of desolation," spoken of by Daniel the prophet, standing in the holy place (whoever reads, let him understand), then let those who are in Judea flee to the mountains (24:9–16).

When Jesus says the gospel will be preached in all the world and then the end will come, we must understand that the Rapture is not the end. When the Rapture happens, there are still seven more years. Then Jesus talks about the Abomination of Desolation that will take place during the Tribulation.

Revelation chapter 14 is also important for this question:

Then I saw another angel flying in the midst of heaven, having the everlasting gospel to preach to those who dwell on the earth—to every nation, tribe, tongue, and people—saying with a loud voice, "Fear God and give glory to Him, for the hour of His judgment has come; and worship Him who made heaven and earth, the sea and springs of water" (vv. 6–7).

This event is during the Tribulation, not before.

The section in the book of Revelation that applies to the Tribulation is chapters 6 through 18. For example, Revelation chapter 14 shows the 144,000 Jews who will be converted and become great evangelists. There is also the angel in Heaven preaching the everlasting gospel to every tribe, nation, and tongue. So I believe any person who has not heard the gospel at the time of the Rapture will certainly hear it from the 144,000 Jews. The Two Witnesses, whom I believe could be Enoch and Elijah but could also be Moses and Elijah, will also have a supernatural ministry on the Temple Mount. Many millions of people will be getting saved (and maybe billions).

The Rapture will be the most evangelistic event in world history. Many, many people will get saved after it happens and during the Tribulation. Again, I believe the Rapture can happen at any moment, and I also believe all of the prophetic events that need to happen have already happened. During the Tribulation, every single human being will hear the gospel supernaturally, but it may not happen before the Rapture.

Questions About ...

Families and Children

God instituted marriage. He alone put the first man and woman together. God also ordained family and gave children as precious gifts to their parents. It is only natural for us to have love and concern for our spouses and children. We receive many questions about what will happen to children at the time of the Rapture. We also hear a lot of concerns about marital and family relationships in Heaven.

God wants us to be in His family. He is a family kind of God, so He cares about your family, your spouse, and your children. He hears your prayers, sees your tears, and is working on your behalf so your loved ones will respond to Him in faith. The Bible does not address some questions about families and the End Times, but we can know about the character of our God. He loves us and cares deeply about the things we care about. It is only right for us to be concerned about our children and families as we think about the End Times.

26

How Do I Talk to Kids About the Rapture?

How should I talk to children and teens about the Rapture without scaring them? I want them to understand its seriousness and importance.

—**Kristina**

I would give three general words of advice:

- Keep it **positive**.
- Keep it **age appropriate**.
- Keep it **biblical**.

My grandchildren know I preach and teach about the End Times. When my granddaughter Kate was around 10 years old, I went for a walk with her one day. She peppered me with questions for about an hour and a half about the End Times. She asked me more questions than most adults have. Some of those were challenging, hard questions. She made her grandfather really think about it all. Even so, I tried to stay very positive as I answered her. I kept telling her, "This is a great thing, Kate. Some bad things will happen in the world, but we are not going to experience the really bad things because Jesus is going to come for us. He's going to take us, and we're going to go to a place that's going to be incredible and beautiful. We're going to be a part of an eternal celebration there."

If children think of the Rapture as a terrifying event that will take them to a scary, unknown place, then it will frighten them. That is why I say we need to be age appropriate in what we share with them. Let them build an interest and ask questions. When children are little, around 4–6 years old, teach them about Jesus and how much He loves them. Teach them the basics of the Bible.

As they mature, they will understand more and be able to ask deeper questions. In my case with my children and grandchildren, I mostly waited for them to start asking questions. Now, I did preach about the End Times often as our kids were growing up. As they listened, they would ask questions, but I was always very positive in my answers. Sometimes they would express their fears. I wanted them to know Jesus is coming for us, and that is a *good* thing for believers. It's going to be so wonderful! Where Jesus is taking us will be incredible. We're going to be with Him forever.

I remember one time when we went out to eat as a family, and my son, Brent, asked from the backseat, "Dad, where does the devil live?" I thought to myself, *Oh my goodness. So now he's thinking about the devil!* Brent started asking a lot of questions about where the devil lives and if he was omnipresent and other questions like those. Your children will challenge you to think about your own beliefs. As a family, we did not have a regular devotional time because we considered every moment to be a teaching opportunity. When we put our kids to bed when they were young, we would pray with them and lead them in a song or two before they went to sleep. However, we also used every moment as a teaching experience. They constantly had questions, and we used every opportunity to teach them about the Bible and the Lord.

I've been shocked by how many teenagers have read my book *Tipping Point*. Parents have told me, "My teen read your book *Tipping Point*. It was extremely encouraging to them because it is written simply, and they can understand it. It contextualizes what they see in the world around them." Teenagers see the craziness in the world today. We need to help them understand, but only to the degree that they are interested.

Many times when young people hear of the Rapture, they will say things like, "Well, I want to graduate from high school," "I want to get married," or "I want to have kids." I understand all those concerns. I felt the same way when I was young. But I need to say this so you can say it to those you love: *When you see Jesus' face, you will never have another regret for all eternity, and you will never look back.* You will not be at the Marriage Supper of the Lamb thinking, *I wish I were at graduation right now* or *I wish I could be having a baby right now.*

When we see Jesus, He will fulfill every desire 10,000 times over. Where we are going is an exquisite place. We will never look back and think we missed anything. That is what I told our children. That does not mean they believed everything I said at the time. They still wanted to hang around and do some things that were important to them. That is natural. But in time they will see how wonderful our hope in Jesus really is.

So I would say again, be very positive, very age appropriate, and very biblical. You can always tell when people are learning about the End Times in the wrong way because they become fearful. Yes, the world is going to get worse and worse just like the days of Noah and Lot according to Luke chapter 17, but Jesus is coming. He will take believers out of this world so we will not go through the Tribulation. We will never see the face of the Antichrist or know who he is. Jesus is going to deliver us from the wrath that is to come (see 1 Thessalonians 1:10). We can comfort our children and others with that knowledge.

Now that our kids are grown and have children of their own, they have said to me many times, "We are so glad you taught us about the End Times." They have also wanted their children to know in an age-appropriate way about the End Times. So just be sensitive and positive. That's the best way to teach them.

27

How Do I Encourage My Teen?

I shared with my 16-year-old daughter your thoughts about the Rapture, and she doesn't see the point of studying or working or for our family to be building a house. She feels overwhelmed. What encouraging words would you suggest for the younger generations who feel they're going to miss out on the things of this life?

—Jason

I get questions like this one quite often. If I were 16, then I would probably feel the same way as your daughter. It would probably bum me out too.

First, as I said in my book *Tipping Point*, we should plan like Jesus isn't coming back for a hundred years but live like He is coming back today. Just plan your life. Get an education, go to school, build a house, and save for retirement. Carry on with life as normal but live like Jesus will come back at any moment. It may be today.

Second, I would remind a young person that they are not living only to go to school. When they get a little older, they are not living only to have babies or work a job. We are living *for Jesus*. The focus of our lives should be on following Him between now and the time He comes. We want to make the biggest difference we can. I don't want Jesus to find me lying in bed doing nothing without any motivation.

You, your daughter, and all of us need to be serving Jesus Christ to the very best of our abilities. Your life is not about serving yourself. If you are living a selfish life, then you are not living for Jesus. Live to influence others to follow Him. Live to build the Church and the Kingdom and do good in Jesus' name. That way of living is both motivating *and* eternal. When you're living for Jesus here in this world, you are amassing treasures in Heaven. Jesus said it this way:

> Do not lay up for yourselves treasures on earth, where moth and rust destroy and where thieves break in and steal; but lay up for yourselves treasures in heaven, where neither moth nor rust destroys and where thieves do not break in and steal. For where your treasure is, there your heart will be also (Matthew 6:19–21).

How do we lay up treasures in Heaven? We do it by serving, giving, and helping other people. That is how we live with eternity in mind.

Third, and this is one of the most important things I will ever say: the instant you see Jesus' face, you'll never think about all the worldly stuff again. You will never have a regret and say, "I never had kids. I didn't get my diploma. I never kissed a boy. I never got married." You are going to be the wife of the Son of God. You will be at an exquisite wedding that lasts for seven years. It will be beyond anything you could ever comprehend. Then you will live for all eternity with a perfect body, a perfect relationship with God, perfect harmony with other people, and a perfect sinless nature. In this life, we hang on tightly to this filthy, evil world. We do so because we can't fully understand what God is getting ready to do for us.

While he was still living, the apostle Paul went to Heaven. In 2 Corinthians chapter 12, he writes,

> I know a man in Christ [Paul speaking of himself] who fourteen years ago—whether in the body I do not know, or whether out of the body I do not know, God knows—such a one was caught up to the third heaven. And I know such a man—whether in the body or out of the body I do not know, God knows—how he was caught up into Paradise and heard inexpressible words, which it is not lawful for a man to utter (vv. 2–4).

Paul saw things that were inexpressible. He says if he tried to describe it, it wouldn't be possible. Paul wanted to be in Heaven with the Lord. In Philippians, he writes,

> For I am hard-pressed between the two, having a desire to depart and be with Christ, *which is* far better. Nevertheless to remain in the flesh *is* more needful for you (1:23–24).

Paul had seen the other side. Once he saw Heaven, he had no fear of death at all. He wanted to go.

Whether you are young, old, or somewhere in between, I can promise that if you saw the other side, then you would be eager for Jesus to return. I completely understand why a young person would feel concerned about the Lord's return or think they should just sit back and wait. Many adults have felt that way through the years. However, I want to say again that we need to live for Jesus right now. We must understand that our lives are for Him and not just for ourselves. We will never have another regret when we see His face.

28 & 29

How Much Should I Say to My Children?

I will answer two related questions:

Question 1: What do you do when your grown children who are saved are being conformed to the things of this world? I believe my grown kids pray, but when I say anything about the Rapture or tell them we are in the end of the End Times, it's as though they think I'm crazy.

—Rachel

Question 2: Can you help me with a Bible, book, or reference to help my teenage daughter become excited for the Rapture? She sees it as the end of her life and can't envision what will come afterward. She says she still has lots of things to do here on earth. It is almost depressing for her to hear about it, like there is no point in living if Jesus is coming soon. I have done my best to encourage her, but it is not really helping.

—Bev

The most important thing is that your children know Jesus Christ as their Lord and Savior. I can't stress that enough. If they know Jesus, then they'll be ready for the Rapture and set for eternity.

Beyond their relationship with the Lord, I would encourage you not to push much. I am saying that because it is very natural for young people to want to get married, have children, and launch a career. They want to experience all the things they've been looking forward to throughout their childhood. So when we say, "Jesus is coming," it crashes the party in their minds.

We have five grandchildren. At Christmastime, we were having a discussion about the End Times with our three older granddaughters. They're all very strong Christians and know a lot about the End Times. All of their lives growing up, they've asked me a million questions, and I've tried to answer every one of them. So naturally we were having a discussion at Christmas about it. And here's what one of my granddaughters said: "I really would like to get married and have children." Then she mentioned other things she wanted to experience before Jesus comes, and the other young women chimed in. I responded that I understood their desires, and maybe they will have those opportunities, but I also believe Jesus is coming very soon.

For those of us who are adults and older, we have the benefit of history, and it gives us a different point of view. Our disposition is different—we want Jesus to come back yesterday. We need to be understanding of young people because they have a different perspective. They don't know all the things we have experienced. We have to be compassionate and listen to their concerns. We don't want to portray the Rapture as a negative thing, as though Jesus is going to crash their party and interrupt their lives.

Jesus will return, and we will be taken up with Him in the Rapture. No believer will regret it. But for young people right now, they can't understand all the wonderful things that will happen when they see the face of Jesus. He will give them perfect bodies and minds. It is beyond their ability to comprehend, and it's beyond ours too. At that moment, no one will say, "I wish I could go back and wear my prom dress, throw that ball one more time, graduate, or have a baby."

So I say let your kids be kids. Let them progress in their faith. They must know Jesus Christ personally. Do everything you can to share His message of salvation with them. Pray for them. Take them to church and help them to know Jesus. If they know Him, then everything will be fine. In my family, we don't try to push too hard because all our grandchildren love Jesus. They all know He is coming, but they also want to experience some things in this life. They are young, and it's completely understandable.

My book *Look Up!* is written for the purpose of helping people to realize the incredible things that are going to happen when we are raptured and fully redeemed by Jesus. It might help your child to read it. Other than that, I don't know of any resource other than Scripture to get your daughter excited about the Rapture. I think time, experience, and the Bible will change her mind eventually. Even if she never changes her mind about the Rapture, the main thing is that she knows Jesus personally. If she is a believer, then I would consider that a major victory and not push too hard for her to change her mind about the End Times.

30

Will I See My Family in Heaven?

Will we be able to find our children and relatives quickly after the Rapture? Also, will we know each other in Heaven?

—Morgan

I get questions like this one a lot. I can tell you everything at the Rapture will be in perfect order. We won't be scrambling around or worried about anything. I believe God will put us in family groups if we have believing relatives who have gone before us, go with us, or come after us. Many times in the Old Testament when someone died, it was said of them that they were "gathered to their people [or ancestors or fathers]" (Judges 2:10; Deuteronomy 32:50). I believe Heaven will be a giant and eternal family reunion. God is an extremely relational God, and I believe the relationships we have on this earth are sacred and eternal to Him.

Will we know each other in Heaven? God is not going to give us a lobotomy. We will not be stumbling around Heaven confused about what is happening. We will know Jesus; that is certain. Here's what Paul says in 1 Corinthians chapter 13:

> For now we see in a mirror, dimly, but then face to face. Now I know in part, but then I shall know just as I also am known (v. 12).

When Jesus comes, we will see Him face-to-face, and we will know Him perfectly as we have been known perfectly by Him. We will also know others as He knows them. In fact, we will know ourselves like we never have before. Did you realize you don't even truly know other people right now? So we might wonder if we will know each other in Heaven, but we don't really know each other right now. We think we do, but we don't. Most of us are very guarded people.

When we get to Heaven, we will finally know everyone. I believe we will know the Bible characters. We will see David, Noah, and Mary. We will know who they are. We will *truly* know them.

Heaven has no shame. There won't be any fear of man in Heaven. We won't have any wounds in Heaven. We won't have the fear of exposure. So as you sit down to talk to someone in Heaven, you will really get to know them. You will talk to that person like never before, person-to-person.

There will be no filters in Heaven. I'm sure you know about all these social media apps that have filters to make people look different than they really do in person. Heaven doesn't have any of those. There's nothing there to bypass or hide.

So I believe that when the Rapture happens, we will be with our loved ones. We will know where they are. Then we will finally know each other as we have been known by the Lord Himself. As the Lord perfectly knows us, we'll be able to know each other.

31

Will All Children Be Raptured?

At the Rapture, will all children be taken, even those of unbelievers?

—Teresa

I absolutely believe that the children of believers will be taken in the Rapture. The reason I believe this is because the conventional teaching among Jews and Bible scholars is that the age of accountability is 13. That is when a Jewish boy goes through a bar mitzvah (son of the law), while Jewish girls have a bat mitzvah (daughter of the law) at around 12. Consequently, around the ages of 12 or 13, Jewish young people historically become responsible for their own decisions, both morally and legally. They become responsible and are thought of as adults. That position would cause concern in Western society, but that is the way the culture was during Jesus' time on earth. So the conventional wisdom in the Jewish society was that God does not hold children under the age of 12 or 13 accountable for their beliefs and actions in the same way adults are supposed to be responsible.

If I came to the average Christian man and woman and said, "Hey, I've got some good news for you: Jesus is going to come next week. I can't tell you the day or the hour, but it will be next week." Most believers would get really excited and say, "Oh my goodness! That is so fantastic!" Then imagine I would say, "But here's the thing—your children aren't going. See your little three-month-old baby over there? You're going to need to find an unbeliever to take care of that baby because the baby can't go." I can't think of a single Christian parent who would say, "Oh, that's great! I'm really excited about going, so I'll just leave the baby here." Any Christian parent I know of would say, "Well, if my children can't go, then I don't want to go either."

When I am asked this question, I can't give a chapter and a verse that directly apply, but I can tell you about the nature of God. It simply doesn't make any sense for Him to take us to the Marriage Supper of the Lamb and expect us to enjoy our time there when at the same time our children are going through Hell on earth under the reign of the Antichrist. So based on the nature of God alone and considering the belief about the age of accountability, I believe young children will go with their believing parent(s). Now, I would encourage parents to lead their children to Christ. If you have children over 13 who are not believers, then I urge you to pray for them and talk to them about following Jesus. Do it lovingly and gently but encourage them to respond to the Lord.

But on the matter of the children of unbelievers, I do not believe they will be taken in the Rapture. Consider what Paul said in 1 Corinthians:

> For the unbelieving husband is sanctified by the wife, and the unbelieving wife is sanctified by the husband; otherwise your children would be unclean, but now they are holy (7:14).

Remember, when Paul first arrived in Corinth, there were no believers. Everyone in Corinth was an unbeliever. Then Paul began to preach the gospel, and some people became believers. There were many cases in which one spouse was a believer, and the other spouse was not. Paul was answering a burning question: what do you do when you're saved, but your spouse is not? Paul instructed the Corinthian believers that if an unbelieving spouse was willing to live with their believing spouse, then they should remain together. The believing spouse's mere presence in the home sanctifies the children and makes them holy.

Paul was stating a very important concept. So what happens when there is a home with no believers? In a case such as that, there's not a spiritual covering for anyone. Consequently, I believe if parents stay on earth at the time of the Rapture, their children will remain with them. Then what happens to the children if one spouse is a believer while the other is not? In that case, I believe the children will go in the Rapture with the believing parent. I believe they are sanctified by the faith of that parent, even if that is the only parent who is saved. Without the presence of a believing parent, children are unsanctified. That is what the apostle Paul was trying to explain to the Corinthian church.

This issue would include single parents who are believers and divorced or separated parents who have full or partial custody of their child or children. Your presence in that child's life is crucial. But for a child who doesn't have a believing parent, I don't believe they will be taken when the Rapture occurs. I realize that there are people who get very emotional concerning this issue because it involves children. I completely understand that, but I would also encourage everyone not to allow their emotions to rise to the level of Scripture. That is a huge mistake.

This is my opinion. I actually hope I am wrong, and God will take all children. I hope I will see all children in Heaven at the Rapture. However, I don't believe we will because I can't find a biblical justification for that belief. I don't see where God has a responsibility to protect an unbeliever's children the way He does the children of believers. One of the great benefits of becoming a believer is coming under God's covering, protection, and blessing.

32

Are There Children in Hell?

You said that unbelievers' children would not go up in the Rapture, but you also said there would be no children in Hell. Can you reconcile those two ideas?

— Teresa

First, I should say there is nothing in the Bible that addresses children going up in the Rapture or children going to Heaven or Hell. When Scripture is silent on an issue such as this, then we have to look at the nature of God. When I'm giving you my opinion, then I'm going to tell you that it's my opinion. That's full disclosure. So let me say clearly: this is my opinion, but it's based on what I know about the nature of God.

I don't believe there is a single child in Hell. I don't think that's the nature of God. But there is an age of accountability, which I believe is somewhere around 13 years old. At that point, God begins to hold people responsible for their own decisions.

I don't think there would be a responsible Christian parent who would want to go in the Rapture but leave their children behind. I don't think God would take the Church but leave Christians' infants, toddlers, and little kids back on the earth to fend for themselves during the worst seven years of human history. So I think believers' children will go with them in the Rapture. I also believe all children who die will go to Heaven.

So what about unbelievers? When Paul first came to Corinth, there were no Christians. Everyone getting saved in Corinth was a first-generation believer. In many cases, one person in a couple got saved, but their spouse did not. So what Paul is addressing here is the question of what if you're married to an unbeliever? What should those new believers do if their spouses don't also follow Jesus? Paul addressed this question:

> But to the rest I, not the Lord, say: If any brother has a wife who does not believe, and she is willing to live with him, let him not divorce her. And a woman who has a husband who does not believe, if he is willing to live with her, let her not divorce him. For the unbelieving husband is sanctified by the wife, and the unbelieving wife is sanctified by the husband; otherwise your children would be unclean, but now they are holy (1 Corinthians 7:12–14).

Paul says a believer's presence in the home has a sanctifying effect on the family. He doesn't mean that an adult is going to be saved simply because they are living with a Christian spouse. In fact, when Jesus talks about the Rapture, He says in many cases one person will be taken and the other left behind (Luke 17:34).

The Rapture is selective; not everyone in a family will go if there are adult unbelievers among them. But according to Paul's exhortation, I believe that believing adults and their children under the age of accountability will go in the Rapture. That's one of the massive benefits of being a believer. You have the knowledge that not only will you be going with Jesus when He comes, but your children are going also.

So if a child is in the home of an unbeliever, then I don't believe that child will be taken in the Rapture simply because they are not in the home of a believer. Then what happens if those children who stay behind die in the Tribulation? I believe they will go to Heaven if they're under the age of accountability. Again, this is my opinion, but I don't think that God holds children responsible if they die until they reach a certain age.

What if that child is in the Tribulation and they reach the age of accountability? Then I think they have a responsibility to put their faith in Jesus. If they don't, then they will be eternally responsible for their decisions. Again, there are things the Bible just doesn't say. I think in situations such as those, we have to rely on the nature of God. That is what I am basing my opinion on. I could be wrong, but as much as possible I am basing my beliefs on God's nature and character.

33

Will I Be with My Family?

Will I be with my spouse and children during the Millennial Reign and in Heaven? Will we know each other? Will babies stay with their mothers?

—Leslie

One of the sayings in the Old Testament when a person died was, "They were gathered to their ancestors" or "gathered to their people." This tells us clearly that Heaven is a place where families are gathered together.

I believe this also includes the Millennial Reign of Christ. Husbands, wives, children, grandparents, aunts, uncles, cousins and families will be eternally joined together in an environment of perfect love. The only condition is for those above the age of accountability to have received Christ.

Regarding the question whether we will know each other or not: Yes, we will finally know each other. We won't float around on clouds with lobotomies. It's not like your mother will be living near you in the Millennium or in Heaven and you won't know her. In fact, you will know each other better than ever before.

You don't really know each other—fully—now. I know that may be a news flash to some people. You *kind of* know each other, but you don't *really* know each other.

Paul writes about eternity in 1 Corinthians:

For now we see in a mirror dimly, but then face to face; now I know in part, but then I will know fully, just as I also have been fully known (13:12 NASB).

That verse is specifically about our relationship with Jesus, but it also applies to us finally being enlightened to what's really going on. I've been married to my wife, Karen, for over 50 years. I know her as well as I can know anyone here on this earth, although she still surprises me sometimes. She knows me as well as she can know me here on this earth, but we still don't know each other—not the way we will in Heaven.

So we will know each other perfectly in eternity, and of course, we will be together as families. You will be there forever with your wife or husband, your kids, your grandkids, your mom, and your dad. What a wonderful reunion it's going to be! We will be together and will finally know each other in a paradise of perfect love and harmony.

There will be no more dying, crying, suffering, sickness, hurt feelings, jealousy, division, or dysfunction. We will finally be able to be together and totally enjoy one another in an endless, joy-filled reunion. It is one of the eternal benefits of knowing Jesus and making Him the Lord of your life!

34

Will Anyone Be Married?

Could you please explain your thoughts about the husband-and-wife relationship once we are in Heaven?
—Charlene

My wife, Karen, has told me many times that I have to live with her in Heaven. She said, "I don't want to see you living with anyone else in Heaven. You have to live with me!" And she's not joking!

So we are married in this life, and our marriages are a representation of Jesus and the Church. That's what the apostle Paul says in Ephesians chapter 5. There is a mystery about human marriage. It really is a picture of our heavenly wedding and our eternal marriage with Jesus Christ. We, as believers, will be with each other and married with Jesus in Heaven. The Church, collectively, will be the wife of Christ, and Jesus will be our Husband. So there will not be the same type of a marriage relationship with our spouses in Heaven that we have here on earth, but our relationship with Jesus and each other will be closer than we can possibly imagine.

The relationships we have in this world are poor substitutes to the relationship we can have now and will have in eternity with Jesus. This world's relationships just really stink in comparison to what we will experience in eternity. The reason I say they stink is because we are fallen. We all deal with selfishness, pride, and our own sinful issues. Sin inhibits our ability to relate to each other.

You may be reading my answer, and you are asking, "So we won't be married in Heaven?" Let me answer your concern. Christian marriages have problems just like everyone else. However, one day Jesus is going to rapture us. We are going to be married to Him. But does that mean you won't know your spouse? Of course not. Your relationship will radically change, and you will be a million times closer to your spouse than you are right now. But our focus will be on our marriage to Jesus, where it needs to be.

I do believe there will be family in Heaven. I have met people who think that going to Heaven is like getting a lobotomy. They think we will wander around aimlessly with no memories. Some people ask, "Will we know each other in Heaven?" The answer is that we will finally and completely know each other. It is right now that we do not know each other.

You will know Abraham, Isaac, and Jacob in Heaven. You will know John, Peter, and Paul. You will know every redeemed person in Heaven. You will know as you are known. You will know Jesus. Finally and forever we will know Him.

I believe we will have close family relationships with our children, grandchildren, uncles, aunts, parents, and other close relatives. We will know each other. I don't know if we are going to live near each other, but it would be just like God for that to happen. If we don't, we will be able to travel at the speed of thought. I don't think family relationships will evaporate when Jesus comes again. We will be married to Jesus, but we will be closer to each other than we could ever possibly be on earth.

Questions About ...

Israel

God chose Israel because of His grace. The Jewish people have been at the forefront of God's plan even before God called Abraham to go to a land he had never seen before. Out of Israel came God's prophets, priests, and kings. The Bible was in the hands of Jewish people before any Gentiles ever found hope and salvation through its words. From the Jewish people came God's Messiah, the Lord Jesus Christ. And from them also came the Church. One hundred percent of the Church was Jewish on the Day of Pentecost when it was born.

Israel is in God's eternal plan. Israel is the super-sign of what God is doing in the End Times. God's final countdown began on May 14, 1948, when He gathered the Jewish people once again to their homeland. Watch Israel, and you will know how close we are to seeing Jesus face-to-face.

A lot of the content on endtimes.com is about Israel. It is necessary for us to tell people what God is doing with the Jewish people and their land. The story would not only be incomplete without Israel, but there also wouldn't be a story. Watch what God is doing in Israel, and you will have a good picture of what God is doing everywhere.

35

Why the Jews?

Why do you think God chose the Jewish people in the first place?

—Joyce

This is what Moses said to the Israelites God delivered from Egypt:

> For you *are* a holy people to the LORD your God; the LORD your God has chosen you to be a people for Himself, a special treasure above all the peoples on the face of the earth. The LORD did not set His love on you nor choose you because you were more in number than any other people, for you were the least of all peoples; but because the LORD loves you, and because He would keep the oath which He swore to your fathers, the LORD has brought you out with a mighty hand, and redeemed you from the house of bondage, from the hand of Pharaoh king of Egypt (Deuteronomy 7:6–8).

It was ***grace.*** God chose the Jewish people simply because of His grace. He chose Abraham because of grace. Abraham was not a perfect man by any means, but God chose him because of grace and love. I don't believe God loved the Jewish people more than He loved other people. He simply chose the Jews to show Himself to all the other nations of the earth. He wanted the nations of the earth to be jealous of Israel so they would also choose Him to be their God.

For example, I was in The Egyptian Museum in Cairo, and a Muslim woman was my tour guide. She took me to an area of the museum dedicated to the era when Joseph would have lived and began:

> "This is Joseph's Pharaoh here in this area, and these are all the arti-
> facts of the Pharaoh Joseph served."
> "You believe in Joseph?"

"Of course, I believe in Joseph. That is our history."

"You believe the Jews lived here in Egypt?"

"Of course I do," she said, "They lived on the delta, the best part of Egypt."

Then I asked, "So you believe Moses led the Jews out of Egypt?"

"The Pharaohs didn't allow any negative words to be written about them. So we don't have a history of the Jews leaving, but we do have a history of Joseph."

"Well, that's very interesting. What happened to the Pharoah Joseph served?"

"He was killed by his priests."

"The Pharaoh was killed by his priests?"

"Yes."

"Why did they kill him?"

"Because he changed gods, and he chose Joseph's God."

You see, Joseph was such a remarkable person in the way he lived his life and the way he served God that this Pharaoh who served other gods chose Joseph's God. That's the way God wanted it to be. The God of Israel wanted the people of Israel to be such a witness for Him all over the earth that the nations would give up their false gods and choose the true God. That is our purpose as Christians. God wants people to see Him in our lives—Jesus in us. When they do, they will become jealous and choose our God. That is why it is so important for us to live properly before a watching world.

36

When Did the End Times Start?

**Why do you believe the End Times countdown began in
1948 as opposed to at the time of the Six-Day War in 1967
when Israel regained control of Jerusalem?**

—**Tammy**

The miracle of Israel happened in 1948. That is when God began
regathering Jewish people from all over the world to the Holy Land.
The Six-Day War was phenomenal, but nothing compared to what
happened in 1948. The prophet Isaiah wrote,

> Before she was in labor, she gave birth;
> Before her pain came,
> She delivered a male child.
> Who has heard such a thing?
> Who has seen such things?
> Shall the earth be made to give birth in one day?
> *Or* shall a nation be born at once?
> For as soon as Zion was in labor,
> She gave birth to her children (Isaiah 66:7–8).

A nation was born in a single day, May 14th of 1948, when the
British mandate ended. Israel declared herself a nation, and
President Truman recognized the status on that very day. Other
nations followed suit, exactly as Isaiah said it would happen.

> It shall come to pass in that day
> *That* the Lord shall set His hand again the second time
> To recover the remnant of His people who are left,
> From Assyria and Egypt,
> From Pathros and Cush,
> From Elam and Shinar,
> From Hamath and the islands of the sea.

He will set up a banner for the nations,
And will assemble the outcasts of Israel,
And gather together the dispersed of Judah
From the four corners of the earth (Isaiah 11:11–12).

That prophetic passage begins with God regathering the Jews. That is what happened in 1948 and not in 1967. I do know some people start the prophetic clock there in 1967, but Israel didn't begin then. That was the reunification of the City of Jerusalem after the June Six-Day War. But Israel began in 1948. It was officially the beginning of the End Times prophetic clock. End Times prophecy has been fulfilled at an alarming rate ever since then.

37

How Can I Support Jewish People?

What is the very best way that I can support the Jewish people? To what organizations that offer effective support for Israel would you recommend sending donations?
—Ephraim

I use an acronym I once saw to help me remember what to tell others who ask what is the best way to support Israel: **P.E.A.C.E.**

P-PRAY

Pray for the peace of Jerusalem, which is something I do daily. Karen and I pray often for Israel.

Pray for Jews to be saved before the Tribulation. According to Zechariah 13:8, only one-third of the Jews will survive the Tribulation. The good news is Jesus will save all the ones who are still living when He returns. They will all be saved in one day. However, the bad news is that many will die first. My prayer is that Jews living today will receive Christ as their Messiah so they won't go through the Tribulation. They will be spared all of those horrible events. They will be raptured with the Church because they will be part of the Church. The Church started with the Jews.

Pray that God would supernaturally protect them all around the world. Ask God to be their Iron Dome, not just in Israel but also all around the world.

Pray for Israel's government to have wisdom. They have a parliamentary government, so their situation can change fairly quickly. So pray for the government.

Pray for the Israeli Defense Forces. Pray that they will be alert and equipped to defend the nation.

Pray for the people and the peace of Jerusalem (see Psalm 122:6). This is something I pray for every single day. I ask for God's blessing on the Jews. And I say again, pray for their salvation.

E-ENGAGE

Engage in friendship; be friends with Jewish people. If you know someone who is Jewish, then befriend them.

A-ASK THEM IN

Ask Jewish people in. Invite them to be a part of your life as much as you can.

C-CONTRIBUTE TO THE GOSPEL

Contribute to organizations and ministries that share the gospel with Jewish people. I recommend a couple that I really like. The first is Daystar (www.daystar.com). Daystar is operated by my dear friends, the Lambs. I know that 100 percent of what someone gives to Daystar for Israel goes directly to Israel. They do phenomenal things in Israel. Second, I can vouch for Jewish Voice, which is led by Jonathan Bernis. He is another friend of mine. Jewish Voice is a very good ministry that preaches the gospel to the Jewish people and offers other kinds of help to them.

E-EDUCATE YOURSELF

Educate yourself about Israel and the Jewish life. Become more informed so that you can be the best witness you can be and the best friend you can be to the Jewish people. Go to trusted news sources and find out what is happening in Israel.

38

Why Does the US Matter to Israel?

I would like to know why it matters what the US says about Jerusalem and Israel.

—Katherine

This is how the Bible records God's covenant with Abraham:

Now the LORD had said to Abram:

"Get out of your country,
From your family
And from your father's house,
To a land that I will show you.
I will make you a great nation;
I will bless you
And make your name great;
And you shall be a blessing.
I will bless those who bless you,
And I will curse him who curses you;
And in you all the families of the earth shall be blessed"
(Genesis 12:1–3, bold mine).

This is God's everlasting promise to Abraham. After the nation of Egypt sentenced the Jews into hundreds of years of slavery, Egypt ceased to be a world power. Babylon did the same thing. Soon they disappeared as a world power. Every nation in history that has mistreated the Jews has ceased to be great, and in many cases they ceased to exist. Look at Nazi Germany. Now 80 years later, Germany still has not recovered its former glory. William Koenig has written a book called *Eye to Eye: Facing The Consequences for Dividing Israel*. It documents 124 specific instances when the

United States has tried to force Israel to divide their land and the historic natural disasters that took place in the US as a result. Look at what God spoke concerning this through the prophet Joel:

> For behold, in those days and at that time,
> When I bring back the captives of Judah and Jerusalem,
> I will also gather all nations,
> And bring them down to the Valley of Jehoshaphat;
> And I will enter into judgment with them there
> On account of My people, My heritage Israel,
> Whom they have scattered among the nations;
> **They have also divided up My land** (Joel 3:1–2, bold mine).

That is a prophecy concerning the times we are living in. God has brought back the captives of Judah and Jerusalem, and He is preparing to gather the nations of the world together at Armageddon to judge them for how they have treated the Jews *and for dividing the land of Israel*!

Right now, the vast majority of the United Nations has come against Israel with the exception of the United States and a few other nations. In the US, we have many problems, but if for no other reason God blesses us because, for the most part, we have stood with Israel since it became a nation in 1948. We were the first nation to recognize their sovereignty. Certain presidential administrations have gone against Israel. I believe the Biden administration is making a huge mistake in trying to divide Jerusalem and force Israel into a two-state solution, which will return the area to pre-1967 boundaries. There are serious consequences when you come against Israel and especially when you force them to give up the precious little land they have. If you have any doubts, I encourage you to read *Eye to Eye*. William Koenig is a journalist and has carefully documented the national consequences for American intervention to try to force Israel to give up its land.

If we bless Israel, then God will bless us. If we curse it, then He will curse us. The American foreign policy related to Israel is absolutely essential. I have profound respect for President Trump's policies related to Israel. I pray for the Biden administration and every administration that follows that they will continue to be pro-Israel.

39

Do Israeli Leaders Understand Prophecy?

Do you think contemporary Israeli leaders take into consideration Old Testament prophecy when they make political decisions? For example, do you think the Gog-Magog War is at the forefront of their minds? Do they understand prophecy the same way Christians do?

—Linda

First, Israel has had five elections since 2019, and due to the shifting political landscape, Israel has had three Prime Ministers since then because the political situation is more fluid than the US political system. Benjamin Netanyahu served from 2009 to 2021 and provided a lot of stability. He was re-elected in 2022 and is the current leader at the writing of this book.

Lapid, the Prime Minister before Netanyahu, was not as devout in the Jewish faith as Bennett, his predecessor. Even so, I am sure most Israeli leaders are very familiar with the Hebrew Bible, our Old Testament. Most Jews aren't just familiar with the Old Testament, but they also memorize parts of the Torah just like Christians learn to memorize Bible verses or passages—especially in childhood. I have no doubt that most political leaders are familiar with the Old Testament prophecies about the Gog-Magog War in Ezekiel chapters 38 and 39.

But I don't know for sure how many decisions are influenced or changed because of what they know about the Bible's prophecies. I have never heard a specific statement to that effect. (It's rare that you'll hear any politician, regardless of their country, referencing "Gog-Magog" in a public statement.)

To answer the rest of the question, however, I believe we can be certain that the Israelis know the Bible. Many are even familiar with the New Testament. When I've visited Israel, my Jewish tour guides have been extremely knowledgeable about the stories of the Gospels, for example.

I believe Israel's understanding of the Bible is one of the reasons they're eventually going to make a preemptive strike on Iran. Persia—or modern-day Iran—is a major participant in the Gog-Magog War, and the Israelis know what the Bible has to say about that event. They also know how important it is to protect their people.

Israel understands Iran's intentions, too, and they know Iran will not hesitate to try to destroy them as soon as they get the chance. As I've said multiple times, I think Israel will act against Iran in the near future. It will happen whether they connect it to Ezekiel's prophecies or not.

40

How Should I Pray for Israel?

When we understand Bible prophecy and what is happening in Israel, how should we pray so we are in line with God's plan, especially since we know war will ultimately break out?

—Lance

The first thing we should do is pray for Jews to be saved before the Tribulation. According to Zechariah 13:8, only one-third of the Jews will survive the Tribulation. The good news is Jesus will save all the ones who are still living when He returns. They will all be saved in one day. However, the bad news is that many will die first. My prayer is that Jews living today will receive Christ as their Messiah so they won't go through the Tribulation. They will be spared all of those horrible events. They will be raptured with the Church because they will be part of the Church once they receive Christ. The Church started with the Jews.

Second, I pray that God would supernaturally protect them all around the world. Ask God to be their Iron Dome, not just in Israel but also all around the world.

Third, pray for Israel's government to have wisdom. They have a parliamentary government, so their situation can change fairly quickly. So pray for the government.

Fourth, pray for the Israeli Defense Forces, Pray that they will be alert and equipped to defend the nation.

Finally, pray for the people and the peace of Jerusalem. This is something I pray for every day. I ask for God's blessing on the Jews. And I say again, pray for their salvation.

41

What About Gentiles?

Luke 21:24 and Romans 11:25 refer to the fullness or the fulfillment of the Gentiles. What does that phrase mean? I have heard someone say that God will turn back completely to the Jews at the Rapture, and Gentiles will no longer be able to be saved. Is that true?

—Brian

This is Jesus in the Gospel of Luke:

> And they will fall by the edge of the sword and be led away captive into all nations. And Jerusalem will be trampled by Gentiles until the times of the Gentiles are fulfilled (21:24).

The phrase "the times of the Gentiles" refers to the period in history when Gentiles (non-Jews) ruled over the city of Jerusalem. That time came to an end in June of 1967 with the Six-Day War. Before that, Gentiles controlled the city or parts of it. In 1948 when Israel became a nation, the Jews ruled the western part of Jerusalem, but the rest of the city was an international no-man's land. So 1967 was the turning point when Israel took complete control over all of the city except the Temple Mount, which is still overseen by Jordanians. When the Jews took over the entire city of Jerusalem, that is when I believe Jesus' words were fulfilled.

This is what Paul says in Romans:

> For I do not desire, brethren, that you should be ignorant of this mystery, lest you should be wise in your own opinion, that blindness in part has happened to Israel until the fullness of the Gentiles has come in (11:25).

The Jews rejected Jesus for the most part, so God has used Gentiles to spread the gospel all over the world. A partial hardening of

Israel's heart doesn't mean no Jews can be saved, but when the time is right, God will restore the entire nation to faith in Him.

As far as God preventing Gentiles from getting saved after the Rapture, the Bible just doesn't teach that. In fact, many people, including Jews and Gentiles, who get saved and will not worship the Antichrist will be martyred and even beheaded during the Great Tribulation. Clearly people will be getting saved during the Tribulation, and that includes Gentiles. In Revelation chapter 7, John writes,

> After these things I looked, and behold, a great multitude which no one could number, of **all nations, tribes, peoples, and tongues**, standing before the throne and before the Lamb, clothed with white robes, with palm branches in their hands, and crying out with a loud voice, saying, "Salvation *belongs* to our God who sits on the throne, and to the Lamb!" All the angels stood around the throne and the elders and the four living creatures, and fell on their faces before the throne and worshiped God, saying:
>
> "Amen! Blessing and glory and wisdom,
> Thanksgiving and honor and power and might,
> *Be* to our God forever and ever.
> Amen."
>
> Then one of the elders answered, saying to me, "Who are these arrayed in white robes, and where did they come from?"
>
> And I said to him, "Sir, you know."
>
> So he said to me, "**These are the ones who come out of the great tribulation**, and washed their robes and made them white in the blood of the Lamb. Therefore they are before the throne of God, and serve Him day and night in His temple. And He who sits on the throne will dwell among them. They shall neither hunger anymore nor thirst anymore; the sun shall not strike them, nor any heat; for the Lamb who is in the midst of the throne will shepherd them and lead them to living fountains of waters. And God will wipe away every tear from their eyes" (vv. 9–17, bold mine).

During the Tribulation, many of those who will not worship the Antichrist and those who have faith in Jesus will be martyred and even beheaded. In John's vison, he says, "These are the ones who come out of the great tribulation." That means they were saved after the Rapture. This is not the raptured Church before the Tribulation.

John's description is how we know the Rapture will be the greatest evangelistic event in the history of the world. I wrote *Where Are the Missing People?* for those who will be left behind at the Rapture. Many thousands of these books have been purchased by Christians to leave in conspicuous places for those who are on earth after Jesus takes the Church to be with Him. I hope that you have bought one or more for that purpose.

Believers are going to be in Heaven. These people who have come out of the Great Tribulation will be from every tribe, nation, tongue, and people. They won't be saved before the Rapture, but God is not through with humanity. He still wants people to be saved. We absolutely know Gentiles will be among those who are saved during the Tribulation. When the Church is raptured out, the lights will come on *in Israel*! When the Church was birthed on the Day of Pentecost, it was 100 percent Jewish. When the Church leaves the earth at the Rapture, 144,000 Jews and the Two Witnesses who are Jewish will preach the gospel around the world. The wonderful story is that salvation came from the Jews. They began it, and they're going to finish it. That's really good news!

42

Do Converted Gentiles Become Jews?

What happens to Gentiles who convert to Judaism? Are they considered Jews or Gentiles?

—Nicole

The Old Testament uses the Hebrew term *gerim* to refer to Gentile proselytes who convert to Judaism, but the term is also used more broadly in the ancient Jewish community. In today's terms, we might call *gerim* guest workers, immigrants, or asylum seekers. God explicitly told the people of Israel to protect well-meaning foreigners and to treat them with justice (Leviticus 24:22). The Lord reminded them that they were once *gerim*, or strangers, in Egypt (Exodus 22:20; 23:9). Abraham even used a form of this word to refer to himself in Genesis 23:4.

The root of the Hebrew word *gerim* is *gyr*, which means to become a resident. The people of Israel were commanded to treat friendly foreigners as neighbors and to provide asylum for them. So when it became common to refer to Gentile converts as *gerim*, the use of the term implied welcoming people outside of the Hebrew community in and offering them both physical and spiritual refuge.

In Old Testament times, there were two types of non-Jewish converts or proselytes in Israel: those who were full-fledged members of the community and those who were not. The first type were Gentiles who had fully embraced Judaism, including the Law and circumcision for males. The second type were Gentiles who accepted some basic tenets of Judaism but not everything, such as circumcision. In the Old Testament, being Jewish was not just a matter of religion; it was also a matter of ethnicity. A Gentile could become ethnically Jewish by fully converting to the religion of Judaism, following all the Law, and by also being circumcised.

In the New Testament era, the status of Gentile proselytes began to change and was not as clear. In Acts chapter 10 we meet Cornelius, a Gentile who feared God and gave alms generously. He also prayed to God regularly (Acts 10:3–4). He was visited by an angel who told him to send for the apostle Peter, who would tell Cornelius what he must do next. When Peter arrived, he preached the gospel to Cornelius and his household, and everyone believed and was baptized (Acts 10:44–48). There is no mention here of their having to become Jews or be circumcised. This meeting between Peter and Cornelius happened before the "Gentile question" was settled for the Church.

Another example of a Gentile convert to Judaism is the Ethiopian eunuch who was a court official of Candace, queen of the Ethiopians (Acts 8:27). He was reading from the prophet Isaiah and became confused (Acts 8:30). Philip explained the passage to him, and the Ethiopian believed in Jesus and was baptized (Acts 8:36–38).

However, in Acts chapter 15, a council of early church (Jewish) leaders convened in Jerusalem to discuss the status of Gentiles who had converted to Christianity. Some of the Pharisees who had become Christians said Gentiles must be circumcised and keep the whole Law of Moses (Acts 15:5). But Paul and Barnabas argued against this requirement (Acts 15:7–11). In the end, the council agreed with each other and the Holy Spirit that the Gentiles did not need to be circumcised or keep the whole Law of Moses, but they should abstain from sexual immorality, idolatry, and eating food sacrificed to idols (Acts 15:20, 29).

So the New Testament church did not require Gentiles who converted to the Christian faith to follow all the practices of Judaism. In the Old Testament, Gentiles would need to become full-fledged Jews in every way, including being circumcised. But in the New Testament, non-Jewish Christians would not need to do this.

Judaism, as it relates to the old covenant, is dead with the coming of Jesus Christ. So Gentiles who have converted to Judaism from that point on are simply Gentiles who have converted to Judaism. Jewishness is genetic. Israel is both a land and a people.

The covenant God made in the Old Testament is to the land of Israel and the people of Israel who are genetic descendants of Abraham. So today, a Gentile who has converted to Judaism is simply a non-Jew who has converted to Judaism as a religion.

For those of us who are Gentiles and saved by coming to Jesus Christ in repentance and faith, God sees us as His chosen people. This claim does not mean God has abandoned ethnically Jewish people. He is also calling them to repentance and faith in Christ. Paul makes this point in his letter to the Romans:

> But it is not that the word of God has taken no effect. For they *are* not all Israel who *are* of Israel, nor *are they* all children because they are the seed of Abraham; but, "In Isaac your seed shall be called." That is, those who *are* the children of the flesh, these *are* not the children of God; but the children of the promise are counted as the seed (9:6–8).

> *What* if God, wanting to show *His* wrath and to make His power known, endured with much longsuffering the vessels of wrath prepared for destruction, and that He might make known the riches of His glory on the vessels of mercy, which He had prepared beforehand for glory, even us whom He called, not of the Jews only, but also of the Gentiles?
>
> As He says also in Hosea:
>
> "I will call them My people, who were not My people,
> And her beloved, who was not beloved."
> "And it shall come to pass in the place where it was said to them,
> 'You *are* not My people,'
> There they shall be called sons of the living God" (Romans 9:22–26).

Christianity came through the Jews first. On the day of Pentecost, Jewish believers in Jesus Christ were gathered. They were all Jews, but they were also "born of the promise." They were "sons of God," which is what Christians are who are Gentiles are now. Now even Gentiles, men, women, and children, can become "sons of God." On the Feast of Pentecost, the day the Church was born, the priest in the Temple would take two loaves of bread and wave them before the Lord, signifying both Jew and Gentile coming into the fullness of God. So, in Christ, Paul says,

> There is neither Jew nor Greek, there is neither slave nor free, there is neither male nor female; for you are all one in Christ Jesus (Galatians 3:28).

A Gentile who becomes a Christian is a "son of God," but a Gentile who converts to Judaism has joined a dead religion because the Law has passed away and does no good whatsoever.

Since Judaism as a religion is dead, does that mean God has given up on Israel? I do not believe in a replacement theology. God's covenant with Israel is eternal (Genesis 15). The real difference between Jews and Gentiles is God chose one of them for a specific purpose. He promised to multiply the Jewish people, give them a land, and bless them forever. God has shaped His entire plan to save humanity around the people of Israel. Through them, we see that God keeps His loving promises to all people. Israel has been chosen for a specific task, and only Israel is chosen for that task.

While I personally am not Jewish, by faith in Jesus Christ, I have become part of God's covenant, and I share Israel's destiny. I am now part of God's plan to show the world what He is like. Before I got saved, I was a stranger to God's covenants of promise (Ephesians 2:12). God has now brought me into His great rescue plan that started with Israel. I am a full heir of God's covenant. I have been grafted into Israel (Romans 11).

God's calling on Israel is irrevocable. It does not depend on Israel's faithfulness but on God's faithfulness. God has not changed His mind. The "New Israel" isn't a different Israel. It simply means that non-Jewish believers are now brought into the family to show the world what the God of Israel is like. God's love for me is greater than anything I can measure, and so is His love for His original chosen people.

In the end, God still has a great plan for His people Israel. The Lord will set His throne in Jerusalem for all the world to see. He will take a stubborn people and change their hearts. Why would I be surprised? He changed mine! Then He invited me to reign with Him in Jerusalem one day.

What, then, will happen to a Gentile convert to Judaism who then becomes a Christian after the Rapture and during the Tribulation?

I think it is wonderful for anyone to come to Christ, although I wish they would have come to Jesus before the Rapture. This is probably a rare example, but I do not believe those people can be considered members of 144,000 Jews prophesied in Revelation who become Christian believers and work to evangelize others (Revelation 7:4). They are still Gentiles and not ethnically Jews, even though they once joined the religion of Judaism. Yes, God will also want them to be saved and remain faithful to Jesus, even at the cost of their lives, but they will not be counted among the 144,000. These Gentiles will be "sons of God" but not counted in the number of Jews. They are still considered Gentiles, but they are also part of God's people and greatly loved by Him.

43

Who Are the Palestinians?

I have heard Palestinians are descendants of the Philistines of the Bible. Is this true?

—Hannah

I've studied this question, and the best biblical scholars say they are not. It's true that the word Palestinian comes from the word Philistine, but that's really where the connection ends.

Archaeologists have found mention of the Philistines in ancient Egyptian records dating to about 1200 BC. These people groups were not from the area of Canaan, and the archaeological evidence confirms that they were not in the region before that time. Most scholars think they came from southern Turkey or Syria, but we can't really know for sure.

So there's probably a little Philistine DNA in some modern-day Palestinians, but the same could be true for any of us. I could have Philistine DNA. You could have it, too. Those people lived a long time ago, and if we go back that far, all of us have billions of DNA relatives.

I'm comfortable saying, as clearly as possible, that the Philistines were very different from modern-day Palestinians.

Whatever the case, Philistines play a major role in the Bible as Israel's main foe during the Old Testament period of the monarchy. They seemed to be advanced in ironmaking, but over time they too fell to other nations, such as the Babylonians and Assyrians. Those who survived intermarried with the Canaanites, who already lived in the region, and the Philistines mostly disappeared as a distinct people.

What did survive is their name and the name of the area where they once lived. The Greeks and Romans both refer to the region as "Philistia."

When Arabs conquered the region in the seventh century AD, they simply adopted the name from the Greeks and Romans. Over time, Philistia morphed into Palestine, and the Arabs who lived there were called Palestinians. There may have been other people mixed in with the Arabs, but modern Palestinians are mostly Arab.

After World War I, the French and British divided the land and adopted the name "Palestine." Anyone who lived there, Arab or Jew, was referred to as a Palestinian by the British. The modern-day movement of Palestinian Arabs as a distinct people really started in the 1920s but has nothing to do with the ancient Philistines.

I suspect the people who are wanting to connect the Philistines— early enemies of the Jews—to modern Palestinians is because they want to portray Arab Palestinians as long-standing enemies of Israel. It's a way to take a shot at them, politically speaking.

We need to be very careful about these kinds of comments or allegations. As I've said repeatedly, I have no quarrel with the Arabs who live in that region. In fact, a percentage of Palestinians are actually Christians! These strong Christian believers are being persecuted by their Arab Muslim neighbors. I believe we should pray regularly for more Arab people to respond positively to the gospel and accept Christ.

I don't have problems with the Palestinian people. My issue is with the Palestinian political movement and its leaders. They oppose Israel. They want to destroy Israel as a nation and Jews as a people. I will always stand against their actions because God opposes their actions.

Now, let me close by saying this: I would also oppose the political leaders of Mississippi, Maine, or Montana if they wanted to do harm to the Jewish people and take over Jerusalem. It's not the people; it's the action of their political leaders.

God never abandoned Israel, and I won't do it either.

Questions About ...

The United States

I love America. I have the deepest love and most sincere prayers for my nation. However, when it comes to Bible prophecy, there's no clear connection between America and the End Times. I respect those who think differently.

Even so, we should pray for our nation, hope for God's intervention, and vote for righteousness. Even if our efforts don't turn the nation around, God is still God, and we are still His people. We should pray and act as though God will have mercy on our country, but understand God is the one who will decide. We will be used for His purposes, and for that we give Him glory.

44

Will the US Matter in the End Times?

What do you think would be God's reason for America not being much of a factor in the End Times?

—Rick

I think the United States will be here when the Rapture happens. We're declining in many ways. China has overtaken the American economy. They're trying extremely hard to overcome us militarily. That's going to take a little while, but they're joining with Russia and other strategic allies. But we are also morally declining. I think America will be basically in the same situation that we're in right now when the Rapture happens, except we will probably see greater moral decline. I don't wish that, but I think that. Too many moral principles are being cast to the wayside.

But when the Rapture happens, it will decimate America. I think there will be other countries that will be greatly affected by the Rapture. Every country will be hit hard to some degree. However, according to research, there are approximately 100 million evangelical Christians in the United States. If we estimate that there are actually 60 to 70 million Americans who are true Christians, then it will take a major toll on the United States. It will overwhelm the American military, educational institutions, healthcare, financial sector, business sector, and government. It will massively weaken the nation overnight in the twinkling of an eye, and it will be almost impossible to recover from it. I just don't think America will be much of a factor for those reasons. We definitely won't be the superpower we are today after the Rapture of the Church.

The good news is you don't see America in End Times prophecy related to the Antichrist and coming against Israel. I just don't think America will be a big deal at that point because of the overall decline of our nation combined with the Rapture. I wish every single American would come to the Lord and be raptured, but I will pray that as many of us as possible will meet Jesus on that day.

45

Does God Punish US Decisions?

Why are random Americans punished for the political attempts to divide Israel's land? Why does God not punish those making the decisions?

—Sheila

As citizens of this nation, we are under the authority of our government. Sadly, just as we suffer for our parents' behavior, we often suffer because of the choices our leaders make. If your parent smokes, then you're going to inhale smoke. If your parent serves poor food, then you're going to be malnourished. If your parent doesn't pay the electricity bill, then the electric company will shut off the lights, even if you weren't the one who neglected the bill. All of those bad things can happen because of a parent's behavior.

We are subject to the consequences of those in authority over us. It doesn't mean that everyone bears the same guilt and punishment. If you're a Christian, submitted to God, and living for Him, then I don't think you will suffer same level of consequences as those who are in open rebellion. But as Americans, we have consequences because of the choices and behavior of our leaders. What the president, the Congress, the Supreme Court, our governors, and other authorities do, we reap some of what they have sown—for good or bad. It's sadly true.

You might say, "But I'm a good person. Why should I be penalized?" It's because you are under the authority of those in leadership over you. I will remind you that this is why I say we should all be voting. And we should all pray for righteous leaders. I understand it might not seem fair to suffer for what our leaders do, but it is reality. We suffer because of the poor decisions of others.

117

46

Is a Revival Coming?

Many contemporary prophets are saying America is headed for revival and some of the Church's best years are still ahead, but when I listen to the *Tipping Point Show*, I get the sense the Rapture and Tribulation are imminent, and there will be no great awakening or widespread revival on the horizon?

—Jared

As I've said elsewhere, I just can't find a Scripture that says there's going to be a great awakening or something like it before the Rapture occurs. I pray for it, and I know many of my fellow believers are praying for the same thing.

The troubling thing is that Jesus said that His coming would be like the days of Noah and Lot. The Bible tells us Noah was a preacher of righteousness. Lot was a righteous man who lived in Sodom and Gomorrah. Lot did not have any converts, and neither did Noah. Now, that's terribly negative. We're supposed to go into all the world and preach the gospel and make disciples. So there are going to be a lot of people getting saved before the Rapture. There is definitely going to be evangelism taking place. But you're talking about a great awakening and a revival in America. I have not heard God say that. If there are prophets out there saying that, then I hope they're right. I pray every single day for an awakening and a revival in America. I love America and care for the nations of the world. The only true hope for America or any nation is Jesus Christ.

But I don't know. I haven't heard the Lord say that to me specifically. And again, I can't find that in the Bible. But I pray it's true.

Questions About ...
The Church

The Church was born on the Day of Pentecost when the Holy Spirit fell upon a gathering of believers. Acts chapter 2 tells this story. The Bible tells us we are the temple of the Holy Spirit, and the Holy Spirit working through the Church is what is restraining sin in the earth right now.

The restraining, therefore, will happen as long as it is supposed to happen and as long as the Church is active. What will stop the restraining? Jesus will remove the Church in the Rapture. Christians will be taken away to be married to Jesus at the Marriage Supper of the Lamb. I am eagerly awaiting that day. Until then, I encourage my fellow believers to remain faithful to the truth, stay in God's Word, and witness like souls depend on it, because they do.

47

Who Is the Bride of Christ?

Why are we, the body of Christ, also referred to as the "bride of Christ"? I cannot find this way of referring to Christians explicitly in the Bible. Revelation 21:9 says the New Jerusalem is the bride. Can you explain?

—Jeanette

Sometimes the Bible speaks explicitly, and sometimes we can gather truth from what the Bible says implicitly. For example, throughout the Old Testament, God speaks of His relationship to Israel as that of a husband to a wife. God is always the Faithful Husband, while Israel is mostly unfaithful. I would specifically draw your attention to prophecies of Jeremiah, Ezekiel, and Hosea.

In the New Testament, however, while the term "bride of Christ" isn't used, the Church is definitely seen as Jesus' bride. In John chapter 14, Jesus said,

> Let not your heart be troubled; you believe in God, believe also in Me. In My Father's house are many mansions; if *it were* not so, I would have told you. I go to prepare a place for you. And if I go and prepare a place for you, I will come again and receive you to Myself; that where I am, *there* you may be also. And where I go you know, and the way you know (vv. 1–4).

In our modern context, we might miss it, but Jesus is using wedding language. He is speaking of Himself as a groom who is going back to His Father's house to prepare a place for His bride, the Church. Jesus is describing what Jewish grooms did when they got married. He was saying when He has finished preparing a place for His bride to live, He's going to come back and receive us, which means He will take the Church as His bride, marry her, and bring her with Him to live forever. Because we don't live in the first century Near East, it's easy for us to miss what Jesus is saying, but to the Jewish minds of that time, they knew exactly what He was saying.

At the Last Supper, Jesus ate with His disciples. He distributed a common cup with wine in it and said, "But I say to you, I will not drink of this fruit of the vine from now on until that day when I drink it new with you in My Father's kingdom" (Matthew 26:29). Jesus was telling His followers that He will drink it with them again in His Father's house. That is the kind of language a Jewish groom would use with his bride when they were betrothed. So, again, this is all wedding language.

In Ephesians, the apostle Paul says,

> Husbands, love your wives, just as Christ also loved the church and gave Himself for her, that He might sanctify and cleanse her with the washing of water by the word, that He might present her to Himself a glorious church, not having spot or wrinkle or any such thing, but that she should be holy and without blemish. So husbands ought to love their own wives as their own bodies; he who loves his wife loves himself. For no one ever hated his own flesh, but nourishes and cherishes it, just as the Lord *does* the church. For we are members of His body, of His flesh and of His bones. "For this reason a man shall leave his father and mother and be joined to his wife, and the two shall become one flesh" (5:25–31).

It seems as though Paul is writing about husbands and wives, and he is, but even more he is speaking about Jesus and the Church. In fact, Jesus says that husbands should treat their wives the same way Jesus treats the Church, His bride.

I will also take you to Revelation chapter 19:

> And I heard, as it were, the voice of a great multitude, as the sound of many waters and as the sound of mighty thunderings, saying, "Alleluia! For the Lord God Omnipotent reigns! Let us be glad and rejoice and give Him glory, for the marriage of the Lamb has come, and His wife has made herself ready." And to her it was granted to be arrayed in fine linen, clean and bright, for the fine linen is the righteous acts of the saints.
>
> Then he said to me, "Write: 'Blessed *are* those who are called to the marriage supper of the Lamb!'" And he said to me, "These are the true sayings of God" (vv. 6–9).

John had a vision of the Marriage Supper of the Lamb. He saw the saints as a whole (the Church) dressed in fine linen, a bridal gown. So, yes, we are the bride of Christ, and our bridal dress is made of our righteous acts, according to John's vision. It is a very clear biblical doctrine. It is one of those important doctrines that might not be mentioned explicitly, but in very graphic language, the New Testament repeatedly refers to Jesus' bride, the Church.

So there is going to be an event called the Marriage Supper of the Lamb. And at the end of it, believers are called Jesus' "wife." We are a bride before the wedding. We are a wife after it. However it happens, it's going to be just an unbelievable event. And in that event, we'll become one with Jesus in a way that we can't even comprehend here. We will be eternally united with the Son of God. It's going to be glorious.

The New Jerusalem is the glorious place we will spend eternity with Jesus. It is described in Revelation chapter 21:

> Then I, John, saw the holy city, New Jerusalem, coming down out of heaven from God, prepared as a bride adorned for her husband. And I heard a loud voice from heaven saying, "Behold, the tabernacle of God *is* with men, and He will dwell with them, and they shall be His people. God Himself will be with them *and be* their God. And God will wipe away every tear from their eyes; there shall be no more death, nor sorrow, nor crying. There shall be no more pain, for the former things have passed away" (vv. 2–4).

The New Jerusalem isn't the bride of Jesus; it is the eternal home of Jesus and His wife, the Church. The emphasis in the text from Revelation 21:2–4 isn't the New Jerusalem. It is God dwelling with us for all of eternity and loving us as we have never been loved before. He will be the ultimate Husband, and we will be His cherished wife.

48

Why Do So Few Teach on the Rapture?

Why do so few Christian churches teach on the Rapture?
—Linda

Most churches are amillennial, which means they don't believe in the literal Millennium or a Rapture of the Church. For example, amillennialism is the official position of the Catholic Church and the Eastern Orthodox Church. Most denominations in America are also amillennial. Revelation chapter 20 say six different times that the Millennium will be 1,000 years long after Jesus returns at the Second Coming. Amillennialism rejects that truth. Despite clear biblical evidence, many Christians and churches choose to allegorize Scripture. They see it as symbolic and not literal. Therefore, they do not believe in a literal interpretation of Bible prophecy, which is hard for me to comprehend.

At endtimes.com, we are dispensationalists. I include myself and Dr. Mark Hitchcock. All of our contributors are dispensationalists, which means we believe in a literal interpretation of Bible prophecy.

Here is an example of how ridiculous an amillennial belief system really is. In 1 Thessalonians chapter 4, Paul is clearly describing the Rapture. There's no symbolism, no allegory, no speculative storytelling. This is a literal text:

> But I do not want you to be ignorant, brethren, concerning those who have fallen asleep, lest you sorrow as others who have no hope. For if we believe that Jesus died and rose again, even so God will bring with Him those who sleep in Jesus.
>
> For this we say to you by the word of the Lord, that we who are alive *and* remain until the coming of the Lord will by no means precede

those who are asleep. For the Lord Himself will descend from heaven with a shout, with the voice of an archangel, and with the trumpet of God. And the dead in Christ will rise first. Then we who are alive *and* remain shall be caught up together with them in the clouds to meet the Lord in the air. And thus we shall always be with the Lord. Therefore comfort one another with these words (vv. 13–18).

Paul is writing about those who died. They are now in the presence of Jesus. Paul uses an idiom or euphemism of the day to talk about those who had died. It is similar to the way we would say someone "passed away." We mean that person has died. In the first century, they would say someone "fell asleep."

The phrase translated "caught up" is derived from the word *harpazo*. It was later translated into Latin as *rapturo*, from which we get the English word *rapture*. There is not one iota of allegorical or symbolic language in that passage. Paul is saying, as a matter of fact, that he received this word from the Lord. God specifically spoke to Paul that He was coming one day to resurrect the dead in Christ and to rapture the living Church. Now Paul was passing this teaching on to the church in Thessalonica. Paul was telling them that this is exactly what will happen. But in spite of this clear teaching of Scripture, most of the Church and Church leaders today disregard it as allegory and reject the truth of the Rapture. But it is a clear scriptural fact!

So I'm hoping our ministry helps to educate pastors and lay people alike about the End Times so they will feel more confident in teaching about it. But I think a lot of pastors just don't know. Many are amillennial. They just don't believe in a literal Rapture or an actual Millennium. If I had to allegorize the Bible, then I might just throw it away. If it's not literal, then why even bother? Why even read it? But it is literal and true. There are places in the Bible and in Bible prophecy where allegory or symbolism are used. But even those areas represent literal truths. We must be careful when interpreting Scripture and Bible prophecy. It must be taken literally unless it is clearly allegorical or symbolic.

49

Does the Church Have to Be Perfect?

I have heard someone say Jesus can't come back yet because He will return for a bride without spot or wrinkle. This person believes the Church has to be perfect before Jesus comes. I have a hard time understanding this opinion because the Bible also says unless He comes back that no one would be saved. Could you help me understand these two passages of Scripture?

—Melissa

I will start with the second Bible reference first. In Matthew, Jesus says,

> And unless those days were shortened, no flesh would be saved; but for the elect's sake those days will be shortened (24:22).

Jesus is talking about how everyone on the face of the earth during the Tribulation would be wiped out physically if He did not come back in the Second Coming, which is different from the Rapture. It is after the Rapture when He will return with all the saints at the end of the Tribulation. Here, Jesus is not referring to spiritual salvation. He is talking about actual physical salvation—it is about saving lives. The world will be in unbelievably bad shape at the end of the Tribulation. The earth would be consumed, and everyone would die if He did not return.

That brings me to the first Bible passage in the question. This is from the apostle Paul:

> Husbands, love your wives, just as Christ also loved the church and gave Himself for her, that He might sanctify and cleanse her with the washing of water by the word, that He might present her to Himself a glorious church, not having spot or wrinkle or any such thing, but that she should be holy and without blemish (Ephesians 5:25–27).

126

These verses are not talking about a perfect church. I hope it is not bad news to anyone that the Church will not be perfect at the time Jesus returns. We are His bride, and He is coming for us as our Bridegroom. Of course, Jesus wants a beautiful bride. He wants a bride without spot, blemish, wrinkle, or anything else like that.

The Word of God in our lives purifies and prepares us for Jesus' return. The degree to which we allow Jesus to minister His Word to us and we receive it into our lives is the degree to which we are prepared to relate to Jesus, both for today and for all eternity. But the truth is that regardless of how discipled, sanctified, or educated we may become, we will still be imperfect until Jesus returns and transforms us to be like Him.

In 1 Corinthians chapter 15, Paul says,

> Now this I say, brethren, that flesh and blood cannot inherit the kingdom of God; nor does corruption inherit incorruption. Behold, I tell you a mystery: We shall not all sleep, but we shall all be changed—in a moment, in the twinkling of an eye, at the last trumpet. For the trumpet will sound, and the dead will be raised incorruptible, and we shall be changed. For this corruptible must put on incorruption, and this mortal *must* put on immortality. So when this corruptible has put on incorruption, and this mortal has put on immortality, then shall be brought to pass the saying that is written: "Death is swallowed up in victory" (vv. 50–54).

This world, including all of us who live here, is corrupted. We will not be completely changed until Jesus returns. It is His grace, blood, and presence that will transform us into perfection. Only then will we be able to relate to Him fully in the eternal sense.

As we live on earth today, the degree that we are submitted to Jesus and receive His Word is how close we will be to Him when He returns. We won't be perfect, but we are in the process of being redeemed into perfection. He will make us perfect immediately when we see Him face-to-face. If someone says Jesus cannot return because the Church is not perfect, then they are missing the point. The Church will never be perfect in this world. We are imperfect people. We live in an evil world in our sinful flesh. It is possible for us to rise above where we are today by God's presence and power in our lives. Even then, we will not become perfect. When Jesus comes, He will make us perfect in the twinkling of an eye.

50

Will the Church Get Stronger?

Does the Bible actually say the Church will rise up and get stronger in the last days? I have been wondering if the Church will be strong and spotless before Jesus returns, or will He make us that way when He comes again?
—Jenny

We, as the Church and as individual believers, will become spotless when Jesus returns. This is how Paul describes it in Ephesians:

> Husbands, love your wives, just as Christ also loved the church and gave Himself for her, that He might sanctify and cleanse her with the washing of water by the word, that He might present her to Himself a glorious church, not having spot or wrinkle or any such thing, but that she should be holy and without blemish (5:25–27).

The degree that we as the Church and as individual believers allow Jesus to minister His Word to us is the degree to which we will be a spotless bride when He comes again. None of us, however, will be perfect until Jesus comes—*none* of us. He is *the only One* who is perfect, and He is the source of our perfection. There is not one Christian or individual church on earth that will be a spotless bride. Only when the Rapture happens will any of us be spotless, and it will happen instantaneously, but not before.

Will the Church, as a whole, become stronger and stronger? I have addressed this question elsewhere. It is my hope and prayer that a great revival and awakening will occur. Daily, I ask the Lord for it. However, I don't have a biblical reference to which I can point that guarantees it in the last days before the Rapture. But the more we allow the Word to do its work in our lives, the more we will be prepared to see Jesus face-to-face. I cannot stress enough how important His Word is in our lives. I may not be completely spotless, but I want to be as close as I possibly can be, so I stay in the Word.

Questions About ...

The Third Temple

Jerusalem is ground zero for the End Times, but more specifically the Temple Mount is a major flashpoint for what will happen near the Rapture and in the early days of the Tribulation. The Temple Mount is the most sacred piece of land in the world for the Jewish people. A major sign of the End Times is preparation for the rebuilding of the Temple in Jerusalem. The Bible mentions four temples that have stood or will stand on the Temple Mount:

1. Solomon's Temple (960 BC)
2. The Temple of Zerubbabel and Herod (538–515 BC)
3. The Tribulation Temple (to be constructed at the beginning of the Tribulation)
4. The Millennial Temple (to be constructed after Jesus' Second Coming)

Jewish groups, such as the Temple Institute, would like to rebuild the Temple immediately, but the Muslim Dome of the Rock stands in the way. The Mount is also home to the Al-Aqsa Mosque, which is the third holiest place in Islam after Mecca and Medina.

The Temple will be rebuilt in Jerusalem, just as the Bible says it will. I don't know exactly when or how the building will take place, but I know it will happen. As we see preparations heating up, as they are right now, we can know the Rapture is closer than ever.

51

Is the Temple Spiritual Only?

I recently heard a Christian author say he believes the location of the Temple has changed from an actual physical structure in Jerusalem to a spiritual building in the heart of believers. He quoted 1 Corinthians 3:16. Do you think the Temple will actually be rebuilt on the Temple Mount? Or is it really a "spiritual temple" like the author suggested?

—John

First, I want to cite the verse the author mentioned: "Do you not know that you are God's temple and that God's Spirit dwells in you?" (1 Corinthians 3:16 ESV).

Second, I want readers to understand that there are many words and phrases in the Bible that have double or even multiple meanings. The verse I cited is one of those examples. Yes, God intimately dwells in us as His temple. The veil or curtain of the Jerusalem Temple was ripped from top to bottom on the day Jesus died on the cross (Matthew 27:51). This curtain separated all of Israel from the most holy place in the Temple. The Spirit of God in His manifest presence dwelled behind that curtain. Because of what Jesus did on the cross, God now makes His temple in the hearts of believers. God was always omnipresent, but because of Jesus' blood, God can intimately dwell with us because of what Jesus' blood purchased for us. That is one way to understand God's temple, but it is not the only way.

When we study Bible prophecy and the End Times, we understand that there will be an actual physical temple rebuilt in Jerusalem. Here is what the apostle Paul says in 2 Thessalonians chapter 2:

Let no one deceive you by any means; for *that Day will not come* unless the falling away comes first, and the man of sin is revealed, the son of perdition, who opposes and exalts himself above all that is called God or that is worshiped, so that he sits as God in the temple of God, showing himself that he is God (vv. 3–4).

This Scripture is referring to when the Antichrist enters a rebuilt Temple in Jerusalem and proclaims himself to be God. That is called the Abomination of Desolation, and it takes place in a rebuilt Temple in Israel, not in our hearts. How could the Antichrist sit in our hearts if the Temple is in our hearts and we have already been raptured three and a half years before the Abomination of Desolation takes place? And by the way, Daniel speaks about the Abomination of Desolation, as do Jesus, the apostle Paul, and the apostle John. So I do not agree with that. I think it is a spiritual truth that we are the temple of the Holy Spirit, but I believe prophetically, there will be a rebuilt Temple to fulfill that Scripture and others as well.

52

Will We See the Temple Rebuilt?

Is it possible the Temple in Jerusalem might start to be rebuilt before the Rapture of believers? Could we actually see it being constructed?

—Tawanna

I personally believe that the Temple will be rebuilt after the Rapture has already occurred, but I could be wrong. There are already many preparations to rebuild being made by The Temple Institute in Jerusalem as well as others. Five perfect red heifers were flown from Texas to Jerusalem in September 2022. A perfect red heifer is necessary according to Numbers chapter 19 to cleanse the Temple Mount as well as the priests to enable them to rebuild and offer sacrifices. It will be another year or so from the writing of this book before we find out if one of the five red heifers remains kosher and qualifies to be the 10th red heifer in Israel's history to be used for ritual cleansing. By the way, the Jews themselves believe the 10th red heifer will usher in the reign of the Messiah. That is exciting!

I believe after the Rapture of the Church that the seven-year covenant the Antichrist confirms with Israel (Daniel 9:27) could pave the way for them to rebuild the Temple. It could be that the Israelis are willing to concede all or part of East Jerusalem to the Palestinians in exchange for the right to rebuild their Temple. But I also believe that the presence of the Two Witnesses on the Temple Mount could protect the Temple builders regardless of what anyone else thinks about it. Remember, the Two Witnesses are hated by the entire world and are killed by the Antichrist in the middle of the Tribulation (see Revelation chapter 11). Protecting the Temple builders and their ability to sacrifice animals could be a lot of the reason they are so hated.

In summary, I just don't believe the world today is ready for Israel to rebuild the Temple. That is an understatement. Just the presence of the Jews on the Temple Mount creates a lot of tension right now. So I believe it is going to take a world-shaking event to create a scenario where Israel is able to rebuild their Temple. My opinion is there will be the Rapture of the Church around the same time as the Gog-Magog War, which is a Russian-led coalition of mostly Muslim nations, including Iran. They will try to destroy Israel, but God Himself will destroy them on the mountains of Israel (see Ezekiel chapters 38–39). In response to this, just as with the Holocaust, there will be international sympathy toward the Jews and a willingness to make concessions to them. This sympathy will open the door for the Antichrist to broker his covenant with Israel, which could possibly include giving them the right to rebuild their Temple.

53

Where Will the Third Temple Be Rebuilt?

Has the location of the new Temple been decided based on the new archaeological discovery of King David's City away from the current Dome of the Rock?

—John

I've read the reports and seen some of the videos that claim new information about the actual Temple location. There are researchers who believe the original Temple, which was built by King Solomon, was located in a different place from what it is commonly believed to be the location today. So here is my answer: When the Temple is rebuilt, the only thing that will matter is what the Jews—the Sanhedrin—believe. They will decide where it's built, and they believe that the Dome of the Rock, a Muslim shrine, sits on the site of the original Temple. The Temple Institute's website makes that claim. They believe that somehow, miraculously, either they must tear down the Dome of the Rock, or an earthquake or some other event will destroy the Dome of the Rock for the Temple to be rebuilt. I'm very impressed by a lot of the reports that come out about the Temple location being different from where people typically think it is. But my default answer is that the only thing that matters is what the Jews believe. So I think it is supposed to be where the Dome of the Rock stands on the traditional site on the Temple Mount.

54

Is Al-Aqsa Mosque in the Way?

Is any portion of the Al-Aqsa Mosque built over real estate that would be needed to rebuild the Temple?

—Kristy

The Al-Aqsa Mosque is actually at the southwest corner of the Temple Mount. It could be in the way according to some archaeologists. Very few excavations have been allowed under the Al-Aqsa. The only one ever carried out there was by a British archaeologist between 1938 and 1942. While the Israeli government controls access to the Temple Mount, the two buildings there, the Dome of the Rock and Al-Aqsa, are controlled by Jordan-based Jerusalem Islamic Waqf. In 2004, the Waqf removed nine tons of dirt from under Al-Aqsa against government regulations and dumped it in the Kidron Valley, claiming it was of no archaeological significance. Since 2004, archeologists have been combing through the soil and have found many important artifacts, including some likely dating to the time of King David. Some scholars believe Israel's priests prepared sacrifices on the site of Al-Aqsa. The Al-Aqsa Mosque is not necessarily the location of the original Temple, but it certainly was adjacent to the Temple where sacrifices were offered. Of greater significance is the Dome of the Rock, according to Jewish experts.

The Dome of the Rock is not technically a mosque; it's just a building recognized as an Islamic shrine. It is the Dome, however, that stands in the way of a new Temple, according to conventional Israeli thinking. I also believe that to be true. There's a significant area to the north of the Dome of the Rock that has no building, and Jews could still build there, but it is not where the previous Holy of Holies rested according to Jewish experts. Many Jewish scholars believe the previous Holy of Holies was precisely on the spot where the Dome of the Rock is now.

Questions About ...

The Gog-Magog War

The stage is being set in the Middle East for the events of the Gog-Magog war. Iran is moving toward nuclear capability, and Israel has vowed not to let that happen. Russia, Iran, and their proxies are gathered on the northern border of Israel. God may use a single provocation as the "hook" in the jaws of Israel's enemies, pulling them into war as promised in Ezekiel chapters 38 and 39. Battle lines have been drawn, and the spark of a single match could set the Middle East—and the world—*on fire.*

It's possible the Rapture has been delayed because world events are still unfolding to set up the Gog-Magog war—or to set up the revelation of the Antichrist. Both of these events could happen in tandem, shortly after the Rapture.

55

Who Will Be Fighting the Gog-Magog War?

What country should we be watching for the Gog-Magog War? I'm not sure which countries are on either side or how it matches Bible prophecy.

—Michelle

Ezekiel chapter 38 is where we see the countries listed:

> Now the word of the LORD came to me, saying, "Son of man, set your face against Gog, of the land of Magog, the prince of Rosh, Meshech, and Tubal, and prophesy against him, and say, 'Thus says the Lord GOD: "Behold, I *am* against you, O Gog, the prince of Rosh, Meshech, and Tubal. I will turn you around, put hooks into your jaws, and lead you out, with all your army, horses, and horsemen, all splendidly clothed, a great company *with* bucklers and shields, all of them handling swords. Persia, Ethiopia, and Libya are with them, all of them *with* shield and helmet; Gomer and all its troops; the house of Togarmah *from* the far north and all its troops—many people *are* with you"'" (vv. 1–6).

- Ezekiel lists Gog and Magog. Gog is a person, while Magog is the land of Gog. It is the area of modern-day Russia. One of Noah's descendants was Gog, and he settled in what today is modern Russia.
- Persia is Iran today. Iranians are not Arabs, but they are Persians.
- We see Gomer and Togarmah, which are located in modern-day Turkey. Some scholars believe Gomer was actually located in modern-day Germany.
- Libya is mentioned by name and is modern-day Libya.

- Ethiopia is also mentioned, but that would include modern-day Sudan and possibly areas of Ethiopia and central Africa.

Many of the areas Ezekiel mentions are Islamic nations today. They are already aligned with Russia and Iran. Mainly we should be looking for what actions Russia and Iran take. They are already closely aligned. Russia has helped build nuclear facilities in Iran. In some ways, they protect Iran and have shared many of their nuclear secrets with them. Many scientists who are working in Iranian nuclear facilities are Russians. Iran is providing many of the weapons for Russia's war against Ukraine. The Russian-Iranian relationship complicates many things on a geopolitical level.

If (or when) Israel bombs Iran, some Russian scientists will die in the process, which will raise the stakes internationally. I wrote about this issue in *Tipping Point*, but the intensity has only grown since then. I believe there is a great likelihood that the Gog-Magog War will begin when Israel bombs Iran. Israel cannot let Iran get nuclear weapons without a significant response. This issue is reaching a boiling point. Iran is enriching uranium fast enough to have nuclear weapons available very soon. It is happening right now.

So Ezekiel lists those countries that will be involved in the Gog-Magog War: Russia, Iran, Turkey (possibly Germany), Libya, Sudan, and possibly areas of Ethiopia and central Africa.

56

Will Damascus Be Destroyed?

What about Damascus? I have heard when it is destroyed, the Rapture happens.

—Melissa

Consider what the prophet Isaiah writes:

The burden against Damascus.
"Behold, Damascus will cease from *being* a city,
And it will be a ruinous heap" (Isaiah 17:1).

What is known as Damascus, Syria today is the longest continually inhabited city in the world. That is why we know that the prophecy in Isaiah chapter 17 about their destruction is yet to be fulfilled. Even though Damascus and that region have a long history of war and conquests, they have never ceased to be a city. That is obvious because of their notable presence today.

But sometime in the near future, some cataclysmic event is going to happen, and they will be destroyed. So when and how will it happen? There are many opinions about that, and what I am about to say is my personal opinion. What I know for certain is that they will be destroyed.

Right now Israel is conducting daily bombing raids in and around Damascus. The reason for this is the Iranians are using the Damascus airport to import their military cargo and munitions in their efforts to entrench themselves in Syria in preparation to destroy Israel. That is their stated objective, and Israel won't stand by idly and let it happen.

So Damascus is now in the crosshairs, and one day someone is going to pull the trigger. Even though their demise could come through an act of God, I believe Israel will destroy them. An example of how this could happen is prophesied in both Psalm chapter 83 and Ezekiel chapters 38 and 39. Here we have two major wars prophesied concerning Israel and their immediate and regional neighbors. I believe both of these wars will be fought around the time of the Rapture and before the Tribulation.

One of the reasons I believe this is because the first three and a half years of the Tribulation will be a time of unprecedented peace in Israel after they confirm their seven-year covenant with the Antichrist. The other reason I believe this is because the second half of the Tribulation is a time of unprecedented danger and war for Israel through which two-thirds of the Jews are killed.

The wars prophesied in Psalm 83 and Ezekiel 38 and 39 are both wars in which Israel wins miraculous victories. But there is a difference in how those victories occur. In the Gog-Magog War prophesied in Ezekiel, God Himself personally defeats the enemies of Israel as He slaughters them on the mountains of the Holy Land as they seek to destroy the Jews. And God rightly gets all of the glory for it.

But in the Psalm 83 war, the Israeli Defense Force (IDF) wins a decisive victory in a war with their immediate neighbors—including Syria. And here is my opinion for how that war will occur. I believe Israel will soon bomb Iran to prevent them from succeeding to acquire nuclear weapons. When they bomb Iran, Israel knows they will be attacked by Iran and their proxies in Gaza, Lebanon, Syria, Iraq, and possibly Jordan. I believe this is the fulfillment of the Psalm 83 war, and I believe Israel will win a miraculous victory over their enemies. In the process, I think it is highly likely that the IDF will use a tactical nuclear weapon to destroy Damascus and deal with that perennial problem decisively.

If the destruction of Damascus doesn't happen then, I believe it will probably coincide with the Gog-Magog invasion of Ezekiel chapters 38 and 39. And I believe both the Psalm 83 war and the Gog-Magog War will happen sometime around the Rapture of the Church. I don't know exactly how or when everything will occur, but I do believe the Rapture and the destruction of Damascus will be in the same season of time.

57

What Role Does the Antichrist Play in the Gog-Magog War?

Doesn't God get the credit for saving Israel from Gog in Ezekiel 38 and 39? How can the Antichrist come in with a peace treaty if Gog-Magog doesn't happen until after the Tribulation starts?

—Mary

Yes, God gets all of the credit for saving Israel from Gog and his coalition of evil nations in Ezekiel 38 and 39. Here is the scriptural proof:

> "I will call for a sword against Gog throughout all My mountains," says the Lord GOD. "Every man's sword will be against his brother. And I will bring him to judgment with pestilence and bloodshed; I will rain down on him, on his troops, and on the many peoples who *are* with him, flooding rain, great hailstones, fire, and brimstone. Thus I will magnify Myself and sanctify Myself, and I will be known in the eyes of many nations. Then they shall know that I *am* the Lord" (Ezekiel 38:21–23).

Whenever the Gog-Magog War of Ezekiel chapters 38 and 39 occurs, God will supernaturally end it with horrific judgment against Israel's enemies in such a manner that the nations of the world won't be able to deny it is the hand of God. I believe this will result in a worldwide sympathy and even support for the Jewish people and the nation of Israel. It is at this point where I believe the Antichrist could very well step onto the world stage and confirm a seven-year peace treaty with Israel. He will in no way get the credit for ending the Gog-Magog War. But he will get the credit for establishing peace in Israel and the Middle East that has been elusive for so long and not possible for any other world leader.

Based on Daniel 9, the Tribulation will begin with the confirming of a seven-year covenant between Israel and the Antichrist. One of the major reasons I believe the Gog-Magog War occurs before the Tribulation is because of the first three and a half years of the Tribulation, Israel is at peace—not at war. And then once the Abomination of Desolation occurs in the middle of the Tribulation, the Great Tribulation occurs, and two-thirds of the Jews die.

The Gog-Magog War will be a supernatural war that God begins by drawing the enemies of Israel to the Holy Land, where He will then annihilate them. It begins with God and ends with God, and not an Israeli is killed. I don't see where anything like this could happen during the Tribulation—though I could be wrong.

58

Why Will Israel Make an Agreement with the Antichrist?

If the Gog-Magog War doesn't happen until after the Tribulation has begun, then what could be the impetus for Israel and the Antichrist's seven-year peace agreement?
—David

Some people say the Gog-Magog War doesn't happen until the end of the Tribulation because of the mention of Gog-Magog in Revelation chapter 20. There John says that when the thousand years of the Millennium have expired, Satan will be released to deceive the nations from the four corners of the earth, and Gog and Magog are mentioned. I believe the Revelation 20 reference to Gog and Magog is an idiom. It is not talking about the Gog and Magog of Ezekiel 38 and 39, because those are very specific regional nations around Israel. They include Russia, Iran, Turkey, Libya, and Sudan. The Gog-Magog reference in Revelation 20 is global:

> Now when the thousand years have expired, Satan will be released from his prison and will go out to deceive the **nations which are in the four corners of the earth, Gog and Magog**, to gather them together to battle, whose number *is* as the sand of the sea (vv. 7–8, bold mine).

As you can see from this text, this isn't the Gog-Magog of Ezekiel 38 and 39, which are defined and limited to a specific region of the earth. This Gog-Magog is referring to "the four corners of the earth." It is global. The Gog-Magog reference here is an idiom linking the spirit of the world at that time to the arrogant and anti-God attitude of the Gog-Magog invaders of Ezekiel 38 and 39.

Dr. Mark Hitchcock believes that the Gog-Magog War will happen near the middle of the Tribulation. I have a great amount of respect for him. As I have said, I believe it happens around the time of the Rapture when the Antichrist confirms a seven-year covenant with Israel. After the Holocaust and World War II, the world had great sympathy for the Jewish people. Where there had been so much antisemitism before the war, after six million Jews were killed, there was worldwide sympathy. The Gog-Magog War will be about an attack from a Russian-led coalition of mostly Muslim nations. Their armies will be killed, but God is going to glorify Himself by protecting Israel. There is going to be a tremendous respect and awe toward Israel that will come out of the Gog-Magog War. That will very possibly set up the seven-year covenant between the Antichrist and Israel.

Several things here could trigger a negotiation if the Gog-Magog War hasn't occurred:

- The promise of the rebuilt Third Temple
- The desire to give East Jerusalem to the Palestinians
- The red heifer may be ready
- The threat of another war.

There may be intense world pressure combined with sanctions against Israel. For example, right now the Biden administration and the United Nations are very supportive of a two-state solution. Netanyahu is very much against it. It could be that there is tremendous pressure coming from all over the world. There could also be the threat of another war. Recently, Israel gave up much of their maritime boundary to Lebanon. But what Israel stated openly was that they didn't want war with Hezbollah. Their terrorism just paid off. The purpose of terrorism is to terrorize others so they give you what you want. They got it. So the threat of war, the promise of a new Temple, or maybe several issues will be combined. It just makes more sense to me that the Gog-Magog War would soften the soil for Israel and lead to the deal with the Antichrist.

Questions About ...
The Rapture

God's next major move will be the Rapture. I believe, and I think the evidence is clear, that it could happen any moment, even while I am writing these words. It is imminent. I'm not setting a date or time, because I don't know exactly when it will happen. I just see the signs, and they all point to the return of Christ in the very near future.

The concept of the Rapture is not foreign to the Bible as some would claim. It is exactly what Paul taught. He comforted the believers in Thessalonica by telling them that all believers will be taken with Jesus when He returns. They don't have to worry about their dead sisters and brothers in Christ. In fact, Jesus will raise them from the dead first. But just a fraction of a second later, He will gather all believers who are still alive. We will have a grand reunion together with the Lord in the air. When Jesus returns, God will set all of His final moves in motion.

59

Why Do We Use the Word "Rapture"?

I have been told that the term "Rapture" is not in the Bible and is a man-made term. Can you explain how that term came to be used instead of saying the "Second Coming"?
—Mary

The New Testament was originally written in Greek. In 1 Thessalonians chapter 4, Paul says,

> We tell you this directly from the Lord: We who are still living when the Lord returns will not meet him ahead of those who have died. For the Lord himself will come down from heaven with a commanding shout, with the voice of the archangel, and with the trumpet call of God. First, the believers who have died will rise from their graves. Then, together with them, we who are still alive and remain on the earth will be **caught up** in the clouds to meet the Lord in the air. Then we will be with the Lord forever. So encourage each other with these words (vv. 15–18 NLT, bold mine).

The Greek word translated "caught up" is *harpazo*. So how do we get the word "Rapture" from that? The word starts in the Latin Vulgate, which was Jerome's translation of the Greek New Testament. We get the word Rapture from the Middle French word *rapture*, which came from Jerome's Medieval Latin word *rapturo*, which means 'to seize hastily, such as in a kidnapping.' That word was derived from an even older Latin word *raptus*, which means 'to carry off.' That answer may seem complicated, but I want people to realize that no one "came up" with this word or "invented" it. It was the normal way to talk about being "caught up" in Latin, which was a language used by a large part of the Church for many centuries after the New Testament times.

Paul says we will be "caught up." *Rapture* is a commonly used word to talk about that event. It's a strictly biblical concept. Paul also says there will be a generation of people who will never die. If you're alive when the Rapture happens, then you will be immediately changed. I believe we are in that generation. The dead in Christ will rise first, but then we who are alive and remain will be "caught up." So we will be seized, caught up, and carried off by Jesus, and it will happen "in the twinkling of an eye." I can hardly wait!

The Second Coming, on the other hand, is a separate event altogether. The Rapture occurs before the Tribulation and is a private event between Jesus and the Church (1 Thessalonians 4; Luke 17). The Second Coming is a very public event that occurs at the end of the Tribulation on the Mount of Olives in Jerusalem, and everyone will see it (Zechariah 14; Revelation 19).

60

Rapture: Different Views?

So many great Christian teachers and leaders have differing opinions about the Rapture and whether those left behind will have an opportunity to receive Christ. Some say the Rapture is before the Tribulation, others in the middle, and still others after. How can people who have studied God's Word so much have such differing views?
—Donovan

I've been studying End Times prophecy for almost 50 years. As a pastor, I have learned people are strongly influenced by their backgrounds. At one time, I was an unsaved heathen. I had no church background. One of the advantages I had was no one ever taught me anything, so I had no preconceived notions about End Times prophecy. I know many people who come from multiple generations of Christians, and they have been steeped in one particular type of End Times theology. That is what they have in their heads, and they can't get it out. They feel allegiance to those beliefs and the people who have taught them. Those teachers might have included their pastors, parents, grandparents, or other loved ones. It's great to be loyal to those you love but not at the expense of truth. Your allegiance should be to the Bible.

A lot of people don't know this about me, since I've studied End Times prophecy a long time, but for about 20 years I believed in a post-Tribulation Rapture. When I first started studying End Times prophecy, it seemed to me to be weak to believe in a pre-Tribulation Rapture—Christians ought to be strong enough to endure anything. That was just my opinion. I thought it would be convenient if we didn't have to go through any trouble, but I believed Christians were going to go through the Tribulation.

I have read hundreds of books about the End Times and studied every prophetic passage of Scripture many times. Over the years, I changed my position and could no longer defend a post-Tribulation Rapture. The evidence against it and for a pre-Tribulation Rapture was so much greater the more I studied. One of the advantages of old guys like me is that we know stuff because we have had time to learn about it. We've studied for a long time. However, just because you have some years on you, and you've studied, doesn't mean you know all the right answers. I don't have a corner on truth, but I also don't have a need to defend something when I find out it is not true. I really don't care as long as it is truth. That means, if we are going to go through the Tribulation, then we're going to go through the Tribulation. We just need to get ourselves ready for it if that's the case.

Nevertheless, I want to be true to the Scriptures. I believe there are people who do not know a lot about the Bible because they haven't really studied it thoroughly. When it comes to End Times prophecy, I have studied the Bible from every angle I know to study. I continue to read books regularly, even those that are against my beliefs. For example, I read a book that came out a couple of years ago. The author himself is a great guy, but everything I don't believe about the End Times is what he believes. I bought his book and read it just to test my own beliefs. After reading it, I was more confident than ever in what I believe.

However, there are other kinds of people. They are not well-studied, and their beliefs are simply not well-formulated. That is one reason I read and listen to older Christian pastors and scholars related to the End Times. There are a lot of great End Times teachers on YouTube and other places. Sadly, some of them have not formulated their beliefs very well.

I am a dispensational theologian. That means I believe in the literal interpretation of Scripture unless a passage is clearly allegorical or symbolic. I believe when the Bible speaks about Israel, it literally means Israel. I believe Israel exists by a special covenant with God. Some people read Israel in the Bible symbolically. This kind of thinking and teaching is a slippery slope. I am aware that many Christians and even pastors interpret the Bible symbolically. A good example is they don't believe the book of Revelation is literal. They think the judgments of Revelation are symbolic. Preterists, for example, believe that the end has already happened in the first several centuries. Others believe the End Times is an ever-evolving situation and can't be understood. But I say for the people who believe in a symbolic interpretation of the Bible that nothing means anything, and anything means anything. I wouldn't read the Bible at all if I didn't think it was literal truth. And honestly, I think a lot of people who don't take it literally don't read it much.

So I believe the only right way to interpret Scripture and End Times theology is literally unless something is clearly symbolic or allegorical. However, when Scripture uses symbolism, it's still telling us something literally is happening, such as with the four horsemen in Revelation chapter 6. So a lot of people can study the Bible and produce a variety of interpretations. Everything depends on how you read and interpret the Bible. Are you a serious student? Or do you just read the Bible casually and then form your beliefs? It makes a huge difference.

61

Rapture: Public or Private?

I hear you say all the time the Rapture will be a private event. Would you be able to point me to the Scripture passages that back that up? By that, do you mean non-believers won't be aware of what's happening? If I were asleep in bed with my spouse at the time, would we see each other being raptured together? Would we be aware of other believers being raptured as well?

—Ray

This is what Paul says in 1 Thessalonians:

> For this we say to you by the word of the Lord, that we who are alive *and* remain until the coming of the Lord will by no means precede those who are asleep. For the Lord Himself will descend from heaven with a shout, with the voice of an archangel, and with the trumpet of God. And the dead in Christ will rise first. Then we who are alive *and* remain shall be **caught up together with them in the clouds to meet the Lord in the air.** And thus we shall always be with the Lord. Therefore comfort one another with these words (4:15–18, bold mine).

Paul says we meet the Lord in the air. That is when we are caught up. In Luke chapter 17, Jesus describes the Rapture:

> "I tell you, in that night there will be two *men* in one bed: the one will be taken and the other will be left. Two *women* will be grinding together: the one will be taken and the other left. Two *men* will be in the field: the one will be taken and the other left."
> And they answered and said to Him, "Where, Lord?"
> So He said to them, **"Wherever the body is, there the eagles will be gathered together"** (vv. 34–37, bold mine).

Not everyone will know what is happening at the Rapture. It is a private event that occurs between Jesus and the Church in the air.

Jesus' Second Coming after the Tribulation is a very public event. People often read verses thinking that they are speaking about the Rapture when they are actually reading about the Second Coming. For example, John writes,

> Behold, He is coming with clouds, and every eye will see Him, even they who pierced Him. And all the tribes of the earth will mourn because of Him. Even so, Amen (Revelation 1:7).

The prophet Zechariah quotes God saying,

> And I will pour on the house of David and on the inhabitants of Jerusalem the Spirit of grace and supplication; then they will look on Me whom they pierced (Zechariah 12:10).

Both of these passages refer to the Second Coming that ends the Tribulation, not the Rapture of the Church. This event could not be more public, while the Rapture is private.

However, I do think we will be aware of other believers being raptured. Unbelievers will not know or understand. So if you are lying in bed with your spouse, and you are both saved, then you would absolutely be aware if you are Christians. You will be going up in the air with Jesus. In fact, I believe you will be together!

62

Rapture: The World's Response?

What will those who are left behind think when we are raptured? Is there a Scripture that indicates how the world will respond to the Rapture?

—Tim

The Bible does not say a lot about how people will respond who are left on earth. However, I do have opinions about what I think will happen. In Matthew chapter 24, Jesus says,

> But as the days of Noah *were*, so also will the coming of the Son of Man be. For as in the days before the flood, they were eating and drinking, marrying and giving in marriage, until the day that Noah entered the ark, and did not know until the flood came and took them all away, so also will the coming of the Son of Man be (vv. 37–39).

Then Paul writes in 2 Thessalonians chapter 2,

> And then the lawless one will be revealed, whom the Lord will consume with the breath of His mouth and destroy with the brightness of His coming. The coming of the *lawless* one is according to the working of Satan, with all power, signs, and lying wonders, and with all unrighteous deception among those who perish, because they did not receive the love of the truth, that they might be saved. And for this reason **God will send them strong delusion, that they should believe the lie,** that they all may be condemned who did not believe the truth but had pleasure in unrighteousness (vv. 8–12, bold mine).

The passage in 2 Thessalonians 2 is about the Antichrist. When the Church is raptured, people will "believe the lie" that is told.

I am not certain what the lie will be, but I have some solid guesses about what it could be. Billy Crone has been a regular guest on the

156

Tipping Point Show. Billy is a former Satanist and New Ager. Before he was saved, he invited spirit guides into his body, not knowing they were really demons. So what the spirit guides said to him is this: "Before long, millions of people will leave the earth. And they are leaving to go into our spaceships." Since the alien belief is very much tied to New Age belief, it made sense to him. The spirit guides said,

> These people that we are going to take are not enlightened, and they are not progressing. They're not evolving the way the rest of you are. So those of you who are on the earth, left on the earth, you're the ones we have chosen. You have evolved, but they will come back to the earth in seven years once we have trained them and gotten them evolved to where they should be.

Imagine the Rapture has happened, and at the same time UFOs appear, and there are "reputable sources" that tell the story Billy heard from the spirit guides. Paul says people will believe—not a lie but **the** lie. Some people think the lie is that the Antichrist is God, which is possible. However, the lie could also be what the demons told Billy Crone. "These people left because they are bad news. They were Christians. They were all people who weren't woke or enlightened and just wouldn't change."

So I don't know exactly what the lie is, but I believe it will be a great shock when a billion or so people disappear. There might be a momentary sort of celebration that makes the people left behind feel good about themselves.

Revelation chapter 6 records the beginning of the Tribulation. By the end of the chapter, the seals are being broken. Rich men, poor men, the free, the slaves, and all these mighty men are hiding in the clefts of the rocks in the caves, saying,

> Fall on us and hide us from the face of Him who sits on the throne and from the wrath of the Lamb! For the great day of His wrath has come, and who is able to stand? (vv. 16–17).

Like in the days of Noah and Lot, there might be scoffing for a time. There might be celebrating for a short season. But shortly thereafter, there is going to be the horrific reality of the Tribulation and judgment that has come upon the earth. And according to

Revelation chapter 7, there will be a mass revival such as the world has never seen.

So I believe there will be a mixture of responses to the Rapture of the Church by those who are left behind. But I believe shock and fear will be most common. And for those who believe "the lie," it may offer them temporary solace. But the hellish reality of the Tribulation will inevitably scare it out of them.

63

What About Donated Organs?

What happens if you've donated organs to someone? Will your body be reunited after the Rapture? What does that mean for someone who has your donated organ?
                                                                —Jamie

Here is what 1 Corinthians chapter 15 says about the transformation of our mortal bodies at the Rapture:

> Now this I say, brethren, that flesh and blood cannot inherit the kingdom of God; nor does corruption inherit incorruption. Behold, I tell you a mystery: We shall not all sleep, but we shall all be changed—in a moment, in the twinkling of an eye, at the last trumpet. For the trumpet will sound, and the dead will be raised incorruptible, and we shall be changed. For this corruptible must put on incorruption, and this mortal *must* put on immortality. So when this corruptible has put on incorruption, and this mortal has put on immortality, then shall be brought to pass the saying that is written: "Death is swallowed up in victory" (vv. 50–54).

The state of our pre-raptured body is unimportant related to the Rapture. It doesn't matter if you have donated organs, lost limbs, are dead and cremated, have been lost at sea, or anything else. God will transform what is left of your corrupted, mortal body and give you an immortal, glorious body better than anything you can presently imagine.

If you have donated organs, then hopefully the recipient was a believer and will be transformed, so the organ won't matter. But if they stay on earth after the Rapture, then I believe the donated organ won't disappear because you won't need it (and they will).

64

Rapture: Souls, Bodies, or Both?

Will our souls rise during the Rapture, or will it be our bodies too? Will a lot of dead bodies be left behind, or will millions of people suddenly be absent?

—Diana

The apostle Paul answers this question:

But someone will say, "How are the dead raised up? And with what body do they come?" Foolish one, what you sow is not made alive unless it dies. And what you sow, you do not sow that body that shall be, but mere grain—perhaps wheat or some other *grain*. But God gives it a body as He pleases, and to each seed its own body.

All flesh *is* not the same flesh, but *there is one kind of* flesh of men, another flesh of animals, another of fish, *and* another of birds.

There are also celestial bodies and terrestrial bodies; but the glory of the celestial *is* one, and the *glory* of the terrestrial *is* another. *There is* one glory of the sun, another glory of the moon, and another glory of the stars; for *one* star differs from *another* star in glory.

So also *is* the resurrection of the dead. *The body* is sown in corruption, it is raised in incorruption. It is sown in dishonor, it is raised in glory. It is sown in weakness, it is raised in power. It is sown a natural body, it is raised a spiritual body. There is a natural body, and there is a spiritual body. And so it is written, "The first man Adam became a living being." The last Adam *became* a life-giving spirit.

However, the spiritual is not first, but the natural, and afterward the spiritual. The first man *was* of the earth, *made* of dust; the second Man *is* the Lord from heaven. As *was* the *man* of dust, so also *are* those *who are made* of dust; and as *is* the heavenly *Man*, so also *are* those *who are* heavenly. And as we have borne the image of the *man* of dust, we shall also bear the image of the heavenly *Man*.

Now this I say, brethren, that flesh and blood cannot inherit the kingdom of God; nor does corruption inherit incorruption. Behold, I tell you a mystery: We shall not all sleep, but we shall all be changed—in

160

a moment, in the twinkling of an eye, at the last trumpet. For the trumpet will sound, and the dead will be raised incorruptible, and we shall be changed. For this corruptible must put on incorruption, and this mortal *must* put on immortality (1 Corinthians 15:35–53).

Jesus was resurrected during the Feast of Firstfruits. Paul says this about Jesus: "But now Christ is risen from the dead, and has become **the firstfruits** of those who have fallen asleep" (1 Corinthians 15:20, bold mine). So Jesus is the firstfruits from the dead—the first person resurrected. Use of this term means whatever happened to Jesus will also happen to His followers; we will be resurrected from the dead just as He was.

When Jesus was resurrected, He walked into the room where the disciples were staying, and He said, "Touch me. Put your hands in my hand. Put your hand in my side. I'm not a ghost. I'm flesh just like you are." Then Jesus sat down and ate with them—real food—and then disappeared (see Luke 24:36–49).

After the Resurrection, Jesus had a supernatural and supranatural physical body that was glorious, and it was just like the ones we will have. People who are dead in Christ, like my dad, have dead bodies. His old, worn-out body that died because of cancer is buried in a casket in Dallas, Texas, under the ground. His spirit is in the presence of Jesus. My dad is not under the ground, but when the Rapture happens, his body will come out of the ground. It is like a seed planted in the ground, and it will shoot out of that ground faster than any plant you have ever seen grow. Then his new body, now glorified by God through resurrection, will be reunited with his spirit, and he will be completely glorified—soul, spirit, and body. The bodies of believers are "sown in dishonor," Paul says, but they will be "raised in power." It is "sown in corruption," but it will be "raised incorruptible." So my dad's body was sown in the ground, but when it comes out of the ground it will be a supernatural, supranatural, and eternal body, just like the body of Jesus Christ.

When Jesus comes in the Rapture, whether a believer is dead or still alive, they will get new, glorified bodies. This promise is one of the greatest in the Bible. We will get eternal bodies that never have pain, sorrow, sickness, decay, or injury. And they will be *physical* bodies. Someone asked me if there would be open graves and empty caskets when the Rapture occurs. I don't know, but wouldn't that be phenomenal? I hope that graveyards are just blown up all over the world. It really would be a great testimony to what has just happened. I can't say for sure, but I hope it's true.

65

Will the Antichrist Be Revealed Before the Rapture?

2 Thessalonians 2:3–4 seems to say the Rapture won't happen until the Antichrist has been revealed, which is supposed to occur in the middle of the Tribulation when he stands on the Temple Mount.

—Janet

A lot of people get confused about this passage. Paul writes,

> Let no one deceive you by any means; for *that Day will not come* unless the falling away comes first, and the man of sin is revealed, the son of perdition, who opposes and exalts himself above all that is called God or that is worshiped, so that he sits as God in the temple of God, showing himself that he is God (2 Thessalonians 2:3–4).

Paul is actually referring to the time in the middle of the Tribulation. This event will spark the Great Tribulation, the worst part of those seven years. Here is what the prophet Daniel says about that time:

> Then he shall confirm a covenant with many for one week;
> But in the middle of the week
> He shall bring an end to sacrifice and offering.
> And on the wing of abominations shall be one who makes desolate,
> Even until the consummation, which is determined,
> Is poured out on the desolate (Daniel 9:27).

The Antichrist will confirm a covenant with Israel at the beginning of the Tribulation's seven years (one week), but they will not understand all of the implications of that agreement. Three and a half years later, he will violate that covenant. At that time, the Antichrist will go into the rebuilt Temple in Jerusalem where he will proclaim himself "God." Note that the Temple does not have to be rebuilt before the Rapture for these things to occur. He will set up an image to himself—which is the "abomination of desolation." Daniel also mentions the Abomination of Desolation in two other places—11:31 and 12:11.

What does "Abomination of Desolation" mean? It is an act that makes the Temple unclean. It is the worst of the worst things that someone could do to show disrespect for the Temple, for Jews, and for God. When the Antichrist declares himself "God," it won't be the first time someone did something awful in the Temple, but it will be the worst. In 167 BC, Syrian ruler Antiochus Epiphanes (Epiphanes means "the Great") set up a statue of a Greek god in the Holy of Holies of Jerusalem's Temple and had a pig sacrificed on the high altar. This event was a foreshadowing of what the Antichrist will do halfway through the Tribulation. Antiochus did his best to insult Israel and her God and stamp out her religion. The Jews gave him a nickname, "Epimanes," which does not mean "the Great." We can roughly translate it as "the madman." Antiochus had the spirit of antichrist, but one is coming who will be much worse. The Antichrist will pollute the new Temple, making it an abomination.

Paul also says,

> For the mystery of lawlessness is already at work; only He who now restrains *will do so* until He is taken out of the way. And then the lawless one will be revealed, whom the Lord will consume with the breath of His mouth and destroy with the brightness of His coming (2 Thessalonians 2:7–8).

An antichrist spirit has been at work in the world since the time Adam and Eve disobeyed God. But the actual Antichrist will be the embodiment and incarnation of Satan himself. The "mystery of lawlessness" is already working in our world, which is an antichrist spirit. Paul says only "He who now restrains will do so until He is taken out of the way." The Holy Spirit in the Church is presently restraining evil, but He will ultimately be taken out of the way when the Church is raptured. Paul then says in verse 8, "And then the lawless one will be revealed." As soon as the restrainer—the Holy Spirit in the Church—is raptured or "taken out," it will be then at the beginning of the Tribulation that the Antichrist will be revealed.

The Church was birthed on the Day of Pentecost when the Holy Spirit came, and the Church became the temple of God. The Spirit lives within us, making us the restrainers of evil within the world. Consider what is happening in the world right now in relation to abortion. Pro-life Christians, ministries, and churches are under a constant onslaught. Christians were working to restrain abortion long before the Supreme Court reached any decision. We are the ones who restrain divorce and other kinds of immorality. Jesus said we are the "salt of the earth" (Matthew 5:13). Jesus was talking about salt as a preservative. Before refrigeration, salt kept food from spoiling and poisoning those who ate it. Without salt on the meat of the day, many people would have died from consuming it. Jesus says we are the preservers, the ones who stop the poison and keep people from consuming things that will harm them.

We are now restraining sin, but when the Rapture of the Church happens, we will be gone with Jesus. Then "the lawless one," the Antichrist, will be revealed. Christians don't know and won't know who the Antichrist is because we will be raptured before he is revealed. That is the reason I don't spend much time speculating about whom the Antichrist will be. I will talk about the character, traits, work, and spirit of the Antichrist, but I don't try to figure out his identity. Believers simply won't know. It's a useless conjecture. And we need to be very happy that we won't know because we won't be here when his reign of terror begins!

66

Will Doubting Christians Be Raptured?

Will Christians who don't believe in the Rapture still be raptured? I have heard some say that if a person doesn't believe in the Rapture, then they won't be caught up. I know some wonderful Christian people who do not believe there will be a Rapture. I do not want them to be left behind!

—Cheryl

It is no secret that I believe in the Rapture. But I don't believe it matters eternally whether or not someone believes in it. God is forgiving, which means He will even forgive some bad theology as long as someone comes to Him in faith, confesses Jesus Christ, and accepts the sacrifice and forgiveness Jesus paid for on the cross. I may be overestimating, but I think most people who will go in the Rapture don't even have a clue that there's going to be one. So many churches and preachers have stopped teaching about the End Times and the coming of the Lord.

I think about my dad as an example. He was very strong Christian before he died, but I don't think he even knew a lot about the Rapture. However, he did know Jesus. You must know Jesus to be raptured—but you don't have to be an End Times expert.

If you know Jesus Christ as your personal Lord and Savior, then you will be raptured. That's all that matters for your eternal destiny. I don't believe someone's theology about the Rapture will matter once we all see Jesus. If someone says, "I can guarantee there's not going to be a Rapture," then it is possible that they could be raptured before they get that sentence out of their mouth. You must know Jesus, but you don't have to know about the Rapture.

Now I think another issue is involved in this question. Believing in the Rapture sure gives believers a lot of comfort in this life. I wrote my book *Look Up!* because I want Christians to know the Rapture is one of the best things we can ever think about. I believe knowing End Times theology and understanding the signs of the times gives us tremendous hope in an incredibly stressful, evil world. If a true Christian doesn't know, then they're going to get raptured anyway. It will be a great day for them whether they believe it or not.

67

Are There Written Materials for People Left Behind?

Do you know of a group addressing what happens after the Rapture, such as putting together materials to be available to those seeking knowledge of God during the Tribulation period?

—**Charity**

My daughter assisted me in creating a great resource for people who will be left after the Rapture. We titled it, *Where Are the Missing People?* Our intention is to guide and comfort people who are going through the most terrifying time in human history. We included an explanation of what has happened and an invitation to accept Jesus Christ. I also included a shorter version of that content in *Look Up!* I believe God wants us to minister to everyone, even those who might not come to Christ until after the Rapture. I would hope they would become Christians before that day, but I want them to know God is still available to them. *Where Are the Missing People?* is not expensive. We wanted to make sure people could leave many copies lying around in conspicuous places. Some people may read it and get saved before the Rapture, but it is mainly for those who are still on earth after it happens. You can buy your copy and get great discounts on bulk orders at store.xomarriage. com or missingpeoplebook.com.

I suggest buying copies to put on your coffee table in your office, somewhere in your home, and in your car. That way once the Rapture occurs, copies will be available for people to find. They will have a full and complete explanation from the Bible about what just happened and what is about to happen. Most importantly, they will be able to know about Jesus and get saved!

68

What Will Happen to Backsliding Christians?

What will happen to backsliding Christians? Will they be left behind if they are not following Jesus at the time of the Rapture?

—**Rita**

The apostle Paul writes,

> For no other foundation can anyone lay than that which is laid, which is Jesus Christ. Now if anyone builds on this foundation *with* gold, silver, precious stones, wood, hay, straw, each one's work will become clear; for the Day will declare it, because it will be revealed by fire; and the fire will test each one's work, of what sort it is. If anyone's work which he has built on *it* endures, he will receive a reward. If anyone's work is burned, he will suffer loss; but he himself will be saved, yet so as through fire (1 Corinthians 3:11–15).

Paul is writing *only* about the judgment of Christians. This is the Judgment Seat of Christ. If a person has Jesus as the foundation of life, then they must choose what they will build upon that foundation. Fire will not destroy gold, silver, and precious stones. They will endure through judgment. The fire is God's scrutiny in judgment. I live my life to serve God and serve and give to others. I live to try to influence others by my example. Those actions are gold, silver, and precious stones. On the day of judgment, when the fire of God tests me, my life will endure though that test because I built with eternal things. I have lived my life for eternity, not for the here and now.

What would happen if I did not live that way? I might be a Christian and sincerely believe in Jesus, but then I live for myself. I didn't do that much for other people. I was selfish. Those actions

169

are wood, hay, and stubble. A person who puts their trust in Christ will get to heaven *yet as through fire.* Some believers will have smoke on their coattails. They will get to Heaven, but the fire will examine how and why they lived their lives. Not much will be left except their salvation.

Do you understand that your life and what you have here on earth are very temporary? God has given you 30, 40, 50, 60, or maybe 100 years. In Heaven we have all eternity, and God is not a socialist. Some people in Heaven didn't have a lot here, but they are fabulously wealthy there for all of eternity. Every believer goes to Heaven as long as they know Jesus. And every believer in Heaven will be incredibly blessed because Jesus is there. He is the foundation, so the wonders of Heaven are vast. However, some people will be extremely rich in Heaven. They will have vast eternal rewards because of the way they live their lives on this earth. Other people will get to Heaven, have Jesus and eternal life, but besides that, they don't have much.

The good thing about Heaven is I think we will be able to share our rewards. I think Heaven will be a wonderful place because we'll all love each other and treat each other well. That is one of the reasons it is Heaven. Sin will be forever gone. There will be no devil to tempt us. And we will all be rich in the love of Jesus!

69

Are We Still in the Final Generation?

Over 70 years have passed since Israel became a nation. Does that mean we are no longer within the confines of what the Bible defines as a generation since the Rapture hasn't occurred yet?

—Jennifer

On May 14, 1948, Israel became a nation. That is when I believe the countdown to the end began. Regarding the End Times and His return, Jesus said,

> Assuredly, I say to you, this generation will by no means pass away till all these things take place. Heaven and earth will pass away, but My words will by no means pass away (Matthew 24:34–35).

The prophet Joel mirrors Jesus' words:

> For behold, in those days and at that time,
> When I bring back the captives of Judah and Jerusalem,
> I will also gather all nations,
> And bring them down to the Valley of Jehoshaphat;
> And I will enter into judgment with them there
> On account of My people, My heritage Israel,
> Whom they have scattered among the nations;
> They have also divided up My land (Joel 3:1–2).

In this text, the prophet Joel is quoting God as saying that in the same period of time when He brings back the captives of Judah and Jerusalem (1948), He will enter into final judgment with the nations of the earth (Armageddon). This text supports what Jesus said in Matthew chapter 24 about a single generation seeing the

End Times play out. So an important question is: How long is a generation? This is what the Bible says:

> The days of our lives *are* seventy years;
> And if by reason of strength *they are* eighty years (Psalm 90:10).

As I write this book, we are 75 years from 1948, so we are a long way into a generation and could be rapidly approaching the return of Christ. I never set dates so I have no idea exactly when Jesus is coming or the end of the age will happen. But in answering this question—yes, we are still within the confines of a generation to which Jesus referred. And I don't believe that is necessarily violated if we go past 80 years. I just believe in the authority of Scripture, and for that reason, I believe we are approaching the end of the generation Jesus was referring to, and the end is very near.

70

Is There Biblical Proof
for the Rapture?

My aunt is a longtime believer, but she says there is no biblical proof for the Rapture. This statement confused me. Is it a common teaching among some Christians that there is no Rapture?

—JC

It is more common than you would expect. Amillennialism teaches that there will be no Rapture. It also teaches that there will not be a literal thousand-year Millennium. In fact, they actually believe we are in the middle of the Millennium right now. They believe that Jesus is ruling the world right now through the Church and that the devil was bound when Jesus was crucified or resurrected. (I don't think he's very bound!) They allegorize biblical prophecy and don't take it literally. Those are just some of their beliefs.

In the first and second centuries, platonic dualism gained a foothold in the Church. Origen, one of the Church Fathers, embraced platonic dualism, and that thought helped to birth the idea of Amillennialism. Church leaders and teachers began to spread the ideas that the Millennium was symbolic, Jesus was spiritually ruling the world through the Church, and the Millennium was already taking place.

My End Times theology is based on dispensationalism, which means I hold to a literal interpretation of the Scripture unless a passage is clearly symbolic or allegorical. I will give a couple of examples. This is what John wrote in the first chapter of Revelation:

> Then I turned to see the voice that spoke with me. And having turned I saw seven golden lampstands, and in the midst of the seven lampstands *One* like the Son of Man, clothed with a garment down to the

feet and girded about the chest with a golden band. His head and hair
were white like wool, as white as snow, and His eyes like a flame of fire;
His feet *were* like fine brass, as if refined in a furnace, and His voice as
the sound of many waters; He had in His right hand seven stars, out
of His mouth went a sharp two-edged sword, and His countenance
was like the sun shining in its strength. And when I saw Him, I fell
at His feet as dead. But He laid His right hand on me, saying to me,
"Do not be afraid; I am the First and the Last. I *am* He who lives, and
was dead, and behold, I am alive forevermore. Amen. And I have the
keys of Hades and of Death. Write the things which you have seen,
and the things which are, and the things which will take place after
this. The mystery of the seven stars which you saw in My right hand,
and the seven golden lampstands: The seven stars are the angels of
the seven churches, and the seven lampstands which you saw are the
seven churches" (vv. 12–20).

John wrote about Jesus' letter to the seven churches. We read about
the seven stars in Jesus' hands and His walking among the seven
lampstands. Clearly this is allegorical or symbolic language. In fact,
Jesus interprets it Himself. He said the seven stars are the angels
of the seven churches, and the seven lampstands are the seven
churches.

Now look at some Scriptures that are literal and specific and not
allegorical. Here is a passage I often refer to from 1 Thessalonians:

But I do not want you to be ignorant, brethren, concerning those who
have fallen asleep, lest you sorrow as others who have no hope. For if
we believe that Jesus died and rose again, even so God will bring with
Him those who sleep in Jesus.

For this we say to you by the word of the Lord, that we who are alive
and remain until the coming of the Lord will by no means precede
those who are asleep. For the Lord Himself will descend from heaven
with a shout, with the voice of an archangel, and with the trumpet of
God. And the dead in Christ will rise first. Then we who are alive *and*
remain shall be caught up together with them in the clouds to meet the
Lord in the air. And thus we shall always be with the Lord. Therefore
comfort one another with these words (4:13–18).

This is the clearest text in the Bible about the Rapture. Notice that
there is not even a hint of symbolism or allegory. It is just a clear
prophecy. It will happen exactly the way that Paul describes it.

Here is a passage from Zechariah 14:

Behold, the day of the LORD is coming,
And your spoil will be divided in your midst.
For I will gather all the nations to battle against Jerusalem;
The city shall be taken,
The houses rifled,
And the women ravished.
Half of the city shall go into captivity,
But the remnant of the people shall not be cut off from the city.
Then the LORD will go forth
And fight against those nations,
As He fights in the day of battle.
And in that day His feet will stand on the Mount of Olives,
Which faces Jerusalem on the east.
And the Mount of Olives shall be split in two,
From east to west,
Making a very large valley;
Half of the mountain shall move toward the north
And half of it toward the south.
Then you shall flee *through* My mountain valley,
For the mountain valley shall reach to Azal.
Yes, you shall flee
As you fled from the earthquake
In the days of Uzziah king of Judah.
Thus the LORD my God will come,
And all the saints with You (vv. 1–5).

This prophecy is mirrored in Revelation chapter 19. It is about the Second Coming of Christ, and it is literal.

One more passage from Acts chapter 1:

Now when He had spoken these things, while they watched, He was taken up, and a cloud received Him out of their sight. And while they looked steadfastly toward heaven as He went up, behold, two men stood by them in white apparel, who also said, "Men of Galilee, why do you stand gazing up into heaven? This *same* Jesus, who was taken up from you into heaven, will so come in like manner as you saw Him go into heaven."

Then they returned to Jerusalem from the mount called Olivet, which is near Jerusalem, a Sabbath day's journey (vv. 9–12).

Jesus ascended to Heaven from the Mount of Olives. His followers stood around in amazement The angels asked why they looked so amazed and then told all the people that Jesus would return the same way He left. He's going to come down, and His feet will touch the Mount of Olives. That is a literal prophecy, and it will happen exactly the way Luke recorded it.

A large portion of churches are amillennial. They don't believe in the Rapture. It is the official position of the Roman Catholic Church, the Eastern Orthodox Church, and many other denominations. Consequently, you will very likely run into many people who believe that the teaching of the Rapture isn't in the Bible. They believe it is symbolic or even nonsense. I am saying it is a huge mistake because the Bible is mostly literal, and so are its prophetic passages. Even when it uses symbolic language, it is referring to actual facts. The Rapture is real, and Scripture is very clear about that.

Questions About ...

The Marriage Supper of the Lamb

Jesus will return at the Rapture, raising the dead in Christ and gathering the living believers. Then He will take all of us together to His Father's house. Jesus said, "In My Father's house are many mansions; if *it were* not *so*, I would have told you. I go to prepare a place for you" (John 14:2).

First, the Rapture occurs, and then a seven-year period begins. On earth, the worst time in human history will be happening—the Tribulation. However, the Marriage Supper of the Lamb will be taking place in Heaven. These two simultaneous events will last for seven years, which is symbolic of a Jewish wedding that takes place for seven days. Jesus will have raptured or resurrected all the believers of all the ages, and then He will marry them as His glorious bride. In those seven years, believers will become Jesus' wife.

71

How Long Is the Marriage Supper?

Is there Scripture to support the idea that the Marriage Supper of the Lamb will last for 7 years? Or is that a theory based off Jewish wedding traditions?

—Julie

The main Scripture is drawn from Revelation chapter 19. There we find the Church is now the wife of Jesus, not the bride. She is presented after the seven years of the Tribulation, so we can deduce the wedding is seven years. In Revelation chapter 4, John says,

> After these things I looked, and behold, a door *standing* open in heaven. And the first voice which I heard *was* like a trumpet speaking with me, saying, "Come up here, and I will show you things which must take place after this" (v. 1).

The first three chapters of Revelation are the revelation of Jesus and His letters to the seven churches. Most theologians believe that the seven churches refer to the Church Age. The Rapture occurs in Revelation 4:1 as John hears a voice like a trumpet calling him to come up to Heaven. The Rapture is connected to trumpets in 1 Thessalonians 4, 1 Corinthians 15, and again in Revelation 4. Then the seven-year Tribulation occurs from Revelation chapters 6 through 18. Then the Church is presented in Revelation 19 as the wife of Jesus, which is when He returns in the Second Coming after the seven-year Tribulation.

That is the main reason most Bible teachers think the wedding lasts seven years. It is taken from the context of the entirety of Revelation. It is also based on the fact that a Jewish wedding is seven days long.

In John chapter 14, Jesus says,

> In My Father's house are many mansions; if *it were* not *so*, I would have told you. I go to prepare a place for you. And if I go and prepare a place for you, I will come again and receive you to Myself; that where I am, *there* you may be also (vv. 2–3).

Jesus is using wedding language, and every Jew would have known that. The bridegroom would leave his father's house, proceed to the bride's house, pay the bride's price, and then return home to prepare a dwelling place for both of them, a *huppa* for him and his bride. Then when the father told the groom it was time, he went to receive his bride and bring her home to the wedding.

So the Jewish wedding does influence the reason we believe the Marriage Supper of the Lamb is seven years long. But it's more than that. It's also the totality of the book of Revelation. The Rapture is at the beginning, the return is at the end, and we have been alone with Jesus during the entire seven years. We begin as a Raptured Church—His bride—and end as His wife.

72

Who Will Get to Go to the Marriage Supper?

If the Marriage Supper of the Lamb occurs during the Tribulation period, then what about those who will be saved during the Tribulation? Will they not get to participate in this wedding of the Lord? Why wouldn't this occur after every enemy has been defeated?

—Ralph

Revelation chapter 19 talks about the Marriage Supper of the Lamb and then vividly describes the physical Second Coming of Jesus. All believers who went in the Rapture, both the living and the resurrected, will be coming with Him. Zachariah 14 gives the same account. Then in Revelation 20, we see the martyrs who were beheaded because of their testimony of Jesus, and they would not worship the Antichrist:

> Blessed and holy *is* he who has part in the first resurrection. Over such the second death has no power, but they shall be priests of God and of Christ, and shall reign with Him a thousand years (v. 6).

The good news is that people who were martyred during the Tribulation will be part of Christ's Millennial Rule. That would also include the people who were saved and then raptured at the Second Coming. Matthew 24:31 clearly says Jesus will send His angels to gather the elect from the four corners of the earth at the time of the Second Coming.

So the second Rapture that occurs at the Second Coming of Jesus includes two kinds of believers who come out of the Tribulation: living believers who were raptured and dead believers who were resurrected. All of these people will become a part of the body of Christ. They will also live and reign with Jesus for 1,000 years. However, they will not participate in the Marriage Supper of the Lamb. It is wonderful that they will be saved and spend the Millennium and eternity with Jesus. Part of the penalty for not receiving Jesus before the Tribulation is that they will not attend the Marriage Supper of the Lamb.

For those of us who have received Christ prior to the Tribulation, we will be honored to be the wife of Christ at the great heavenly wedding. Jewish weddings of the time lasted seven days, so the seven years of the Marriage Supper of the Lamb corresponds to each of those days. The years will run consecutively with the Tribulation. That is a valuable benefit those who receive Christ before the Tribulation will get to enjoy.

The purpose of the Tribulation is for God to pour out His wrath and punish a world in rebellion to Him. People who get saved during the Tribulation will miss the Marriage Supper of the Lamb. But I don't believe they will in any way be second class citizens of the Kingdom of Heaven. They will be one with the Church and Jesus Himself. They will also be His wife as they rule and reign forever with Jesus and with us.

I realize there are those who believe the Marriage Supper of the Lamb will occur after the Second Coming and at the beginning of the Millennium. I think the best argument they have is because Jesus would want to include in the ceremony those who got saved during the Tribulation. I can understand that argument.

The main problem I have with it is that the Marriage Supper of the Lamb is announced before the Second Coming, and we, the Church, are presented as Jesus' wife. I personally believe the seven years of the Tribulation correspond to the seven years of the Marriage Supper of the Lamb. During those years, we are marrying Jesus, and at the end of that time we have consummated our relationship with Him and are prepared to return with Him to rule and reign.

73

Will There Be Any Sorrow at the Marriage Supper?

If we were raptured before the Tribulation, wouldn't it seem kind of strange for us to be in Heaven having a seven-year feast, laughing and enjoying ourselves with Jesus and other believers while the Tribulation is occurring on the earth? How could we truly enjoy that feast when so many people are getting slaughtered?

—Jeff

First, I want to say that nothing wrong is happening. It may feel wrong to think about that possibility, but it's not. What will be happening on earth is *justice*. Finally after 2,000 years of grace—and even more if we consider how gracious God was before the Incarnation—His wrath is loosed on the world. Jesus was mocked and slapped, and people spat in His face. His Name has become a curse word for many people. Millions have rejected Jesus and shown outright hostility toward Him. But finally, all of His bottled-up wrath will come to the surface. Jesus has waited as long as He can. He's been patient, but the world keeps getting worse and worse. He is about to take His followers out of the world to where we will attend the greatest wedding of all time, the Marriage Supper of the Lamb. Meanwhile, wrath will be poured out on the world.

Justice will come. People will be getting what they should have gotten a long time ago. Revelation calls it "the wrath of the Lamb":

> And the kings of the earth, the great men, the rich men, the commanders, the mighty men, every slave and every free man, hid themselves in the caves and in the rocks of the mountains, and said to the mountains and rocks, "Fall on us and hide us from the face of Him who sits

on the throne and from **the wrath of the Lamb**! For the great day of His wrath has come, and who is able to stand?" (6:15–17, bold mine).

People on earth will be experiencing the Lord's righteous indignation and judgment.

Second, when weddings take place on earth, people still get murdered as they are happening, and others starve to death. Horrible things happen while wedding celebrations are being held all the time. We are just not aware of it—*because we are at a wedding*. Even if we know bad things happen all the time, we block those out of our minds because weddings are special events. When we are at the most important wedding of all time, I don't think we will have an awareness of awful events on earth. How could we celebrate in Heaven for seven years yet be horrified with the conditions of the world? It would be like attending a wedding and having *Terminator: Judgment Day* showing on screens all around us. I don't think we will be aware of that because Jesus won't let anything ruin His wedding.

I don't believe people on the earth have any idea what is happening in Heaven at the time either unless they're believers. Revelation chapter 12 also tells us that Satan will get thrown completely out of Heaven during the Tribulation. People wonder why God would let Satan in His presence in the first place. God created him, so he does have limited access to Heaven until he is thrown out in Revelation 12. Why does God throw Satan completely out of Heaven? I believe it is because God doesn't want Satan to be there for the Marriage Supper of the Lamb any more than you would want your worst enemy to be at your wedding. So Satan and his evil minions will be cast out of Heaven, and Heaven will be prepared for the Marriage Supper of the Lamb.

Just remember that everything happening on the earth is righteous and just. God in His grace has withheld His wrath. But for seven years, He will take us to the Marriage Supper of the Lamb, and all Hell will break loose on earth. We will be married to Jesus for all eternity at the Father's house. The Father's house is described in Revelation chapters 21 and 22, and it is more beautiful than anything we can imagine. Jesus said,

In My Father's house are many mansions; if *it were* not *so*, I would have told you. I go to prepare a place for you. And if I go and prepare a place for you, I will come again and receive you to Myself; that where I am, *there* you may be also (John 14:2–3).

Jesus is there right now at the Father's house. He's going to return and rapture us. He will take us back to His Father's house.

Questions About ...

The Tribulation and the Antichrist

The Tribulation isn't just judgment. It is the wrath of God Almighty upon a world that has rejected Him and rebelled against Him. Even though there will be people saved during the Tribulation, it will be the worst time in human history, and Jesus said unless those days would be cut short, no flesh would survive.

During this time, the Antichrist will emerge. He will lead the world to worship himself! This "man of lawlessness" will take "his seat in the temple of God, proclaiming himself to be God" (2 Thessalonians 2:3–4). Ultimately, Jesus will return with all the saints at His Second Coming. The Antichrist will be defeated and thrown into the lake of fire.

Paul tells us to comfort one another with the wonderful truth that Jesus will deliver us from wrath. He will deliver us from the Antichrist. There is no possible way you can comfort me by telling me I will go through the Tribulation and the terror of the Antichrist. I want to offer comfort to believers. We are not destined for the wrath of the Lamb; we are destined for the Marriage Supper of the Lamb. While the world goes through seven years of Hell on earth and the Antichrist has his reign of terror, believers will be going through seven years of delight and blessing in the presence of Jesus.

74

Is Pre-Tribulation Belief Destructive?

I recently heard a preacher say that pre-Tribulation belief was "destructive." I personally believe what you teach about Noah and Lot because that's what the Bible says, but what would you say when people call that belief destructive?

—Roman

As I've said on the *Tipping Point Show* and previously in this book, I was post-Tribulation in my beliefs for about 20 years. I'm approaching 50 years of studying Bible prophecy. When I first started hearing about the Rapture, I believed Jesus would come at the end of the Tribulation. I felt like the people who believed that Jesus was coming before the Tribulation were wimps. I really did. I felt like believers were going to go through some hard times. And it is true that Jesus never promises us that we won't go through hard times. I thought that was just the way it is, and the Tribulation would not be something we would escape.

However, the more I read and studied about the End Times, the more I found I could no longer support that position. I didn't simply change my mind because I found suffering unpleasant. In fact, I would have kept that position if it were supported in the Bible. I believe pastors say that pre-Tribulation teaching is destructive because they don't think Christians are ready to face real suffering. But I need to say there's no way for anyone to fully prepare for the Tribulation. It will be worse than anyone can imagine. The one way to prepare for the Tribulation is to get ready to die, because over half of the world's population will not survive it.

The Tribulation will be the worst time in human history. There will be a massive evangelistic outreach carried out by the 144,000 Jews of Revelation chapters 7 and 14, but it will enrage the Antichrist. He will murder those new believers en masse.

In 1 Thessalonians chapter 5, the apostle Paul writes,

> For God did not appoint us to wrath, but to obtain salvation through our Lord Jesus Christ (v. 9).

Suffering through the Tribulation is not in our future. Jesus says,

> Watch therefore, and pray always that you may be counted worthy **to escape all these things** that will come to pass, and to stand before the Son of Man (Luke 21:36, bold mine).

Jesus was speaking specifically about the Tribulation. If you really understand the Bible and the Tribulation, then I honestly think it's emotionally destructive to tell people that they will have to go through those things.

In the previous chapter in 1 Thessalonians, Paul also wrote, **"Therefore comfort one another with these words"** (4:18, bold mine). I really believe that End Times prophecy is comforting when you hear it properly taught. It's for our encouragement and not our terror. So I don't believe we're going to be here during the Tribulation. I believe we're going to be taken by Jesus in the Rapture, because He's going to deliver us from the wrath that is to come.

75

Will Unbelievers Have
a Second Chance?

Does it say anywhere in the Bible what happens to the non-believers who go to Hell before the Tribulation? I've always thought during the Tribulation people would get a second chance to redeem themselves and be saved. Would all the unbelievers come back to earth during the Tribulation to get a second chance too?

—Lindsay

No, the unbelievers who are now dead are in Hell. They are not coming back. Living people who are here during the Tribulation will certainly get a chance to receive Christ. I believe hundreds of millions if not billions of people will get saved during the Tribulation. The bad news is they will have to live through the Tribulation and the reign of the Antichrist. The good news is they will have an opportunity to be saved.

What happens to unbelievers when they die? Jesus gave an actual account of what happens. This is not a parable:

There was a certain rich man who was clothed in purple and fine linen and fared sumptuously every day. But there was a certain beggar named Lazarus, full of sores, who was laid at his gate, desiring to be fed with the crumbs which fell from the rich man's table. Moreover the dogs came and licked his sores. So it was that the beggar died, and was carried by the angels to Abraham's bosom. The rich man also died and was buried. And being in torments in Hades, he lifted up his eyes and saw Abraham afar off, and Lazarus in his bosom.

Then he cried and said, "Father Abraham, have mercy on me, and send Lazarus that he may dip the tip of his finger in water and cool my tongue; for I am tormented in this flame." But Abraham said, "Son, remember that in your lifetime you received your good things, and likewise Lazarus evil things; but now he is comforted and you are tormented. And besides all this, between us and you there is a great gulf fixed, so that those who want to pass from here to you cannot, nor can those from there pass to us."

Then he said, "I beg you therefore, father, that you would send him to my father's house, for I have five brothers, that he may testify to them, lest they also come to this place of torment." Abraham said to him, "They have Moses and the prophets; let them hear them." And he said, "No, father Abraham; but if one goes to them from the dead, they will repent." But he said to him, "If they do not hear Moses and the prophets, neither will they be persuaded though one rise from the dead" (Luke 16:19–31).

I will say again, this is a true story. There was an unnamed rich man and a beggar named Lazarus who would sit at the gate of this wealthy man's property. The rich man never lifted a finger to help Lazarus in his hunger and misery. They both died and went to Abraham's bosom, which is in the center of the earth. This place for the dead was actually made up of two locations that were very close together: (1) Paradise or Abraham's bosom, which was like a "pre-Heaven" and (2) Hades, another name for Hell. The rich man was in the hellish section, while Lazarus was with Abraham in the heavenly section. The rich man looked across a chasm that was fixed between them. He saw Lazarus resting in the arms of Abraham, and he said, "I'm in torment. Let him come and dip his finger in the water and cool off my tongue. I'm miserable." Abraham replied, "We can't pass back and forth between these two places. You're on that side, and we're on this side. You had all your good things in your earthly life, but you took God's blessings for granted. Lazarus suffered greatly in the world, but now he's in Paradise."

So when non-believers die, they go to Hell. According to the Bible, Hell is down in the center of the earth. Then where is Heaven? In the Old Testament, it was Abraham's bosom. Where is it now? The apostle Paul answers,

> But to each one of us grace was given according to the measure of Christ's gift. Therefore He says:
>
> > "When He ascended on high,
> > He led captivity captive,
> > And gave gifts to men."

(Now this, "He ascended"—what does it mean but that He also first descended into the lower parts of the earth? He who descended is also the One who ascended far above all the heavens, that He might fill all things) (Ephesians 4:7–10).

Paul is saying that Jesus took the people on the Paradise side with Him to Heaven. He descended into the lower parts of the earth to get them, and then He ascended with them.

The apostle Paul gives even more description in 2 Corinthians chapter 12 when he talks about his own visit to Heaven:

I know a man in Christ who fourteen years ago—whether in the body I do not know, or whether out of the body I do not know, God knows—such a one was caught up to the third heaven. And I know such a man—whether in the body or out of the body I do not know, God knows—how he was caught up into Paradise and heard inexpressible words, which it is not lawful for a man to utter (vv. 2–4).

What is the third Heaven? The first heaven is the atmosphere around us. The second heaven is outer space. The third Heaven is the presence of God in Heaven. So Jesus led captivity captive. He descended into the lower parts of the earth. It means He took the righteous people who were there in Abraham's bosom and took them with Him to the third Heaven where they are now.

So when people died in the Old Testament and went to Heaven, it means they went to Abraham's bosom, which was in the center of the earth. Now when unbelievers go to Hell, it is still the center or lower parts of the earth. However, Jesus moved Heaven. Now when a believer dies, they will go into the presence of God in Heaven, into the third Heaven. That's where believers are who have died. Their bodies may be dead on earth, but their spirits are alive in the presence of God.

During the Tribulation period, when people die they will go to Hell down in the earth. Believers will go to Heaven. The good news is a lot of people will be saved during the Tribulation, which is a beautiful thing.

So when we die, we will go to one of those two places—Heaven or Hell. Our eternal destination is decided by our choice to accept

Jesus and to make Him the Lord of our lives, which I hope every-one reading this has done. That is how people get saved and spend eternity in Heaven. But after death, there is not another choice like that for anyone.

76

Who Are the 144,000 Jews?

As you teach about the 144,000 Jews after the Rapture, it sounds like they will immediately start evangelizing. If they are believers, then how are they still present after the Rapture?

—Sam

The 144,000 witnesses will be present by God's design. He will call them for that purpose. So when the Church is raptured, they will be here on assignment. The Bible specifies their role. In Revelation chapters 7 and 14, we discover why they will be here.

Here is what is written in Revelation chapter 7:

> After these things I saw four angels standing at the four corners of the earth, holding the four winds of the earth, that the wind should not blow on the earth, on the sea, or on any tree. Then I saw another angel ascending from the east, having the seal of the living God. And he cried with a loud voice to the four angels to whom it was granted to harm the earth and the sea, saying, "Do not harm the earth, the sea, or the trees till we have sealed the servants of our God on their foreheads." And I heard the number of those who were sealed. One hundred *and* forty-four thousand of all the tribes of the children of Israel *were* sealed (vv. 1–4).

At this point, John goes into detail about the witnesses that will come from Israel's twelve tribes.

Then John describes a massive harvest of souls that come from the witness of the 144,000:

> After these things I looked, and behold, a great multitude which no one could number, of all nations, tribes, peoples, and tongues, standing before the throne and before the Lamb, clothed with white robes, with palm branches in their hands, and crying out with a loud voice, saying, "Salvation *belongs* to our God who sits on the throne, and to

the Lamb!" All the angels stood around the throne and the elders and the four living creatures, and fell on their faces before the throne and worshiped God, saying:

"Amen! Blessing and glory and wisdom,
Thanksgiving and honor and power and might,
Be to our God forever and ever.
Amen."

Then one of the elders answered, saying to me, "Who are these arrayed in white robes, and where did they come from?"

And I said to him, "Sir, you know."

So he said to me, "These are the ones who come out of the great tribulation, and washed their robes and made them white in the blood of the Lamb. Therefore they are before the throne of God, and serve Him day and night in His temple. And He who sits on the throne will dwell among them. They shall neither hunger anymore nor thirst anymore; the sun shall not strike them, nor any heat; for the Lamb who is in the midst of the throne will shepherd them and lead them to living fountains of waters. And God will wipe away every tear from their eyes" (vv. 9–17).

All of these events are described in chronological order. The 144,000 witnesses are directly responsible for all the huge harvest of souls being saved. The angel seals the 144,000, which means they are then anointed and bulletproof. God protects them through all of the things that are going on in the world. Then we see a multitude from every nation, tribe, and tongue standing before God's throne. This is about the people who are saved during the Tribulation. They got saved and then were killed either in a judgment on the earth or by the Antichrist. The multitudes are so large that they cannot be counted. This is the greatest awakening the world will ever know. So many people will be saved, and these new believers are linked directly to the 144,000.

Revelation chapter 14 also makes a direct connection to the 144,000:

Then I looked, and behold, a Lamb standing on Mount Zion, and with Him one hundred *and* forty-four thousand, having His Father's name written on their foreheads. And I heard a voice from heaven, like the voice of many waters, and like the voice of loud thunder. And I heard the sound of harpists playing their harps. They sang as it were a new song before the throne, before the four living creatures, and the elders; and no one could learn that song except the hundred *and* forty-four thousand who were redeemed from the earth. These are the ones who were not defiled with women, for they are virgins. These are the ones who follow the Lamb wherever He goes. These were redeemed from *among* men, *being* firstfruits to God and to the Lamb. And in their mouth was found no deceit, for they are without fault before the throne of God.

Then I saw another angel flying in the midst of heaven, having the everlasting gospel to preach to those who dwell on the earth—to every nation, tribe, tongue, and people (vv. 1–6).

In Revelation 7, the 144,000 preach the gospel, and multitudes are saved. Then in Revelation 14, they are mentioned in a direct connection to the gospel being preached. These witnesses will be amazing evangelists who supernaturally spread the gospel all over the earth during the Tribulation. These are the Bible passages where we get these facts.

77

What Do the Two Olive Trees and Two Lamp Stands Represent?

What is your take on the two olive trees and the two lamp stands?

—Trey

These are the verses you are referring to in Revelation:

> These are the two olive trees and the two lampstands standing before the God of the earth. And if anyone wants to harm them, fire proceeds from their mouth and devours their enemies. And if anyone wants to harm them, he must be killed in this manner. These have power to shut heaven, so that no rain falls in the days of their prophecy; and they have power over waters to turn them to blood, and to strike the earth with all plagues, as often as they desire (11:4–6).

I believe this prophecy refers to Enoch and Elijah. Some people believe they will be Moses and Elijah because they are the ones who met Jesus on the Mount of Transfiguration (Matthew 17:1–13; Mark 9:2–8; Luke 9:28–36). I would not quibble with them, but Enoch and Elijah never died. God took Enoch (Genesis 5:24). Then Elijah went up in a chariot of fire (2 Kings 2:11). Moses experienced death. I think it would be very unusual for God to send Moses back to die again because these Two Witnesses will be killed by the Antichrist—but I could be wrong.

So the two olive trees and the two lampstands specifically refer to the Two Witnesses. They will know Jesus intimately. They are fulfilled Jews, which means they are Messianic. Enoch and Elijah or Moses and Elijah will return preaching the full gospel of God. The entire world despises them. Later in Revelation chapter 11, the Antichrist kills them (vv. 7–10). Then he will have their dead bodies laid in the street in Jerusalem for three days. The entire world will celebrate and send gifts to each other to commemorate their deaths (vv. 11–13).

These are followers of Jesus. They are preaching the gospel, and everybody hates them, but no one can do anything about it. These men are literally untouchable until three and a half years into the Tribulation.

78

Who Is the Antichrist?

Who is the Antichrist? Does the Antichrist know who he is?

—Dina

I really don't think the Antichrist knows who he is. Judas robbed money from Jesus. He was ambitious and was expecting Jesus to take over the government or something like that, thus making him rich and powerful. When a revolution didn't materialize, Judas became disillusioned. I believe he was motivated by thinking he would ascend to power with Jesus. When he realized it wasn't going to happen, he turned Jesus over to the authorities—he betrayed the Lord.

Here is one of the most chilling passages in the Bible:

> Then Satan entered Judas, surnamed Iscariot, who was numbered among the twelve. So he went his way and conferred with the chief priests and captains, how he might betray Him to them. And they were glad, and agreed to give him money. So he promised and sought opportunity to betray Him to them in the absence of the multitude (Luke 22:3–6).

So Satan entered Judas. Demons are disembodied spirits. So Satan is able to spiritually enter a person, and that can only happen if that person is devoid of God. God and Satan can't coexist.

So the Antichrist is going to be a man completely devoid of God. He's going to be against Jesus, against the Word of God, and a completely godless man. I don't believe he knows who he is, at least not yet. I think at this point he is an open and willing vessel for Satan, who will enter him just like he did Judas. He's obviously going to be an extremely ambitious man and someone dead set against the Word of God.

Some people wonder if the Antichrist will really be a human. I believe he is. The apostle Paul writes this about him:

> Let no one deceive you by any means; for *that Day will not come* unless the falling away comes first, and the **man of sin** is revealed, **the son of perdition**, who opposes and exalts himself above all that is called God or that is worshiped, so that he sits as God in the temple of God, showing himself that he is God (2 Thessalonians 2:3–4, bold mine).

The apostle Paul in this text refers to the Antichrist as a "man" and a "son." Therefore I don't believe he is angelic or extraterrestrial as some believe. This is a very sinful man, but I believe he will be a human being just like Judas. Satan will supernaturally empower him. He will be a human who has been hijacked by Satan.

The book of Daniel says the Antichrist will be a king with fierce features (Daniel 8:23). I don't know whether he will be handsome or not. He will probably be more scary than handsome. His life will be full of intrigue. He will be a very charismatic person and a brilliant politician. Once Satan fully enters the Antichrist, he will become Satan incarnate. He's the whole bad package who will emerge on the world's scene.

I do believe he is born and is alive right now. Some people think there has always been someone the devil had waiting in the wings to be the Antichrist. Remember, the devil isn't all-knowing. Therefore, he doesn't exactly know when the end will come. So he always has evil people ready.

I believe that the real Antichrist is already in the world today, and I believe he is an adult. I believe he is in a position of influence and ready to step onto the world scene. I say this because I don't believe we are just living in the last days; I believe we're living in *the last of the last days.*

I don't know how long it will take the Antichrist to ascend to power. I think he is in the process of ascending already. It will be a satanically supernatural rise to world leadership. It will not be by normal means. I don't know how long it will take for him to confirm a seven-year peace covenant with Israel, but I think it will be close to the timing of the Rapture and the Gog-Magog War. I'm not sure about all the details, but that seems to be the right timing.

79

How Will the Antichrist Confirm the 7-Year Peace Agreement?

How do you see the seven-year peace agreement being generated? What position of authority would the Antichrist be in for him to sign it without being obvious that it is him?

—David

The Bible does not say that the Antichrist signs or makes a treaty or agreement. He either confirms or approves something that has already happened. He will have to be in some kind of a governmental position, especially related to Israel, because this is a formal covenant he is making with them.

This is the prophet Daniel describing the evil reign of the Antichrist:

Thus he said:

"The fourth beast shall be
A fourth kingdom on earth,
Which shall be different from all *other* kingdoms,
And shall devour the whole earth,
Trample it and break it in pieces.
The ten horns *are* ten kings
Who shall arise from this kingdom.
And another shall rise after them;
He shall be different from the first *ones*,
And shall subdue three kings.
He shall speak *pompous* words against the Most High,
Shall persecute the saints of the Most High,

And shall intend to change times and law.
Then *the saints* shall be given into his hand
For a time and times and half a time
But the court shall be seated,
And they shall take away his dominion,
To consume and destroy *it* forever.
Then the kingdom and dominion,
And the greatness of the kingdoms under the whole heaven,
Shall be given to the people, the saints of the Most High.
His kingdom *is* an everlasting kingdom,
And all dominions shall serve and obey Him" (Daniel 7:23–27).

This passage is talking about the Antichrist and his global reign during the Tribulation. The reason I included that full text from Daniel is that at the end is the completion of the story of the Tribulation. Jesus returns at the Second Coming, and the saints rule and reign with Him during the Millennium.

A beast (the Antichrist) will rise up with 10 kings under him. The Antichrist will subdue three kings, but then he will rule over these 10 kingdoms. We know from Daniel 9 that he will arise from a revived Roman Empire. That area includes what today would be the European Union, parts of the Middle East, and Northern Africa.

In my opinion, the Gog-Magog War will coincide with the Antichrist's rise to power. Some devastating event will happen, which is going to give him the opportunity to confirm his covenant with Israel. In the middle of the Tribulation, he will go into the Temple and proclaim himself God and speak pompous words against God. That is the Abomination of Desolation.

80

Is the Mark of the Beast Unforgiveable?

Can a person repent after taking the Mark of the Beast? I've heard both sides of the argument: (1) if you take the Mark of the Beast, then you have chosen death and can't go back, or (2) if you take it, then you can repent and still be saved. What are your thoughts?

—Zillow

I do not believe those who take the Mark of the Beast can repent. I also do not think anyone will take it accidentally; it is something willful. Someone who takes it will basically renounce God and the teachings of Scripture. The Mark of the Beast is the Antichrist's mark, so people will know what they are doing. John describes it in Revelation chapter 14:

> Then a third angel followed them, saying with a loud voice, "If anyone worships the beast and his image, and receives *his* mark on his forehead or on his hand, he himself shall also drink of the wine of the wrath of God, which is poured out full strength into the cup of His indignation. He shall be tormented with fire and brimstone in the presence of the holy angels and in the presence of the Lamb. And the smoke of their torment ascends forever and ever; and they have no rest day or night, who worship the beast and his image, and whoever receives the mark of his name."
>
> Here is the patience of the saints; here *are* those who keep the commandments of God and the faith of Jesus (vv. 9–12).

When John records that certain saints remain patient and keep God's commands, he is referring to the Tribulation. Believers will have to patiently endure, refuse the Mark of the Beast, and keep their faith. So I do not believe there will be an opportunity for repentance or salvation for anyone who receives it. It is an unfor-giveable sin for which many will pay an eternal price.

Believers alive today will not have to be concerned about the Mark of the Beast. They will be taken in the Rapture, so the Tribulation will not be part of their experience. This is one of the reasons why we should understand the End Times. Knowing about them gives us great comfort.

81

Who Makes Up the Great Multitude?

Who is the "Great multitude which no one could number, of all nations, tribes, peoples, and tongues," from Revelation chapter 7? Verse 14 says they came out of the Tribulation. Will there be more people saved after the Rapture than before it?

—Lorens

Here is the selection of Scripture from Revelation chapter 7:

After these things I looked, and behold, a great multitude which no one could number, of all nations, tribes, peoples, and tongues, standing before the throne and before the Lamb, clothed with white robes, with palm branches in their hands, and crying out with a loud voice, saying, "Salvation *belongs* to our God who sits on the throne, and to the Lamb!" All the angels stood around the throne and the elders and the four living creatures, and fell on their faces before the throne and worshiped God, saying:

"Amen! Blessing and glory and wisdom,
Thanksgiving and honor and power and might,
Be to our God forever and ever.
Amen."

Then one of the elders answered, saying to me, "Who are these arrayed in white robes, and where did they come from?"

And I said to him, "Sir, you know."

So he said to me, "These are the ones who come out of the great tribulation, and washed their robes and made them white in the blood of the Lamb. Therefore they are before the throne of God, and serve Him day and night in His temple. And He who sits on the throne will dwell among them. They shall neither hunger anymore nor thirst anymore; the sun shall not strike them, nor any heat; for the Lamb

206

who is in the midst of the throne will shepherd them and lead them to living fountains of waters. And God will wipe away every tear from their eyes" (vv. 9–17).

When the Rapture occurs, the greatest revival in the history of the world will take place. The Tribulation begins in Revelation chapter 6 and goes through the Four Horseman of the Apocalypse and the Seven Seals being broken. Revelation 7 is the next chapter, and so evidently when the Rapture occurs and the wrath of God begins to be poured out, there is a massive worldwide revival. When John writes about it, he says, "These are the ones who have come out of the great tribulation," The word translated "out" is the Greek word *ek.* It means 'leaving in the midst of something.' So this event in Revelation 7 is right in the midst of the Tribulation. John is not giving a picture of people who were saved before the Rapture; this is the people who are getting saved *after* the Rapture.

So will more people get saved after the Rapture than before it? I don't know how to give an exact number, but it will be a massive number of people who get saved. I think it may be up to a billion people or more. John says they will come from all over the world, and the number will be huge: "A multitude which no one could number." It will be an amazing sight to see.

82

Why Does Armageddon Happen?

Why is there an army forming toward the end of the Tribulation, and why is there the war of Armageddon if the Antichrist reigns and apparently has the upper hand?
—Susan

The apostle John writes about this time in Revelation chapter 19:

> And I saw the beast, the kings of the earth, and their armies, gathered together to make war against Him who sat on the horse and against His army (v. 19).

According to Revelation chapter 13, the Antichrist will have absolute authority over all nations, tribes, and tongues with one glaring exception: the Jews will not give up Jerusalem. Right now, the United Nations and several individual countries keep trying to divide the nation of Israel and the city of Jerusalem even further. Benjamin Netanyahu is rightfully a hardliner on this issue. He has said repeatedly, "Jerusalem is the indivisible and eternal capital of Israel." I agree with him and so does God.

So the Antichrist will not have control of Jerusalem, and it will enrage him. Armageddon will happen because the Antichrist, his armies, the United Nations, and their armies will march on Israel in an effort to destroy them and solve the Israel problem permanently. That is what Armageddon will be about.

How do I know Armageddon will be about Jerusalem? The prophet Zechariah explains:

> The burden of the word of the LORD against Israel. Thus says the LORD, who stretches out the heavens, lays the foundation of the earth, and forms the spirit of man within him: "Behold, I will make Jerusalem

a cup of drunkenness to all the surrounding peoples, when they lay siege against Judah and Jerusalem. And it shall happen in that day that I will make Jerusalem a very heavy stone for all peoples; all who would heave it away will surely be cut in pieces, though all nations of the earth are gathered against it" (Zechariah 12:1–3).

Zechariah chapters 12 through 14 tell us very clearly that Jerusalem will become the focal point for the Antichrist's final hostility. Look what is happening right now. Struggles between Hamas and Israel are not about Gaza. It is about Palestinian control and access to parts of Jerusalem. In 2022, Hamas became enraged that Jewish police were limiting the number of Muslims in Jerusalem during Ramadan. The Israeli authorities limited the numbers of people who could enter the area of the Temple Mount. Muslims were angered also that inhabitants of the Sheikh Jarrah neighborhood in East Jerusalem were evicted. A fight over Jerusalem started that conflict. Nothing significant was happening in Gaza. It was about Jerusalem.

I bring this up to illustrate that Jerusalem will be ground zero for Armageddon. It is the problem no one can solve, the cup of drunkenness that makes everybody crazy, and the heavy stone no one can move. The Antichrist won't be able to solve it either. His final solution will be to come with the armies of the world in an effort to destroy the Jews and claim complete global domination. He will fail. Jesus will return with us and destroy the Antichrist and those with him.

Now I saw heaven opened, and behold, a white horse. And He who sat on him *was* called Faithful and True, and in righteousness He judges and makes war. His eyes *were* like a flame of fire, and on His head *were* many crowns. He had a name written that no one knew except Himself. He *was* clothed with a robe dipped in blood, and His name is called The Word of God. And the armies in heaven, clothed in fine linen, white and clean, followed Him on white horses. Now out of His mouth goes a sharp sword, that with it He should strike the nations. And He Himself will rule them with a rod of iron. He Himself treads the winepress of the fierceness and wrath of Almighty God. And He has on *His* robe and on His thigh a name written:

KING OF KINGS AND
LORD OF LORDS.

Then I saw an angel standing in the sun; and he cried with a loud voice, saying to all the birds that fly in the midst of heaven, "Come and gather together for the supper of the great God, that you may eat the flesh of kings, the flesh of captains, the flesh of mighty men, the flesh of horses and of those who sit on them, and the flesh of all *people*, free and slave, both small and great."

And I saw the beast, the kings of the earth, and their armies, gathered together to make war against Him who sat on the horse and against His army. Then the beast was captured, and with him the false prophet who worked signs in his presence, by which he deceived those who received the mark of the beast and those who worshiped his image. These two were cast alive into the lake of fire burning with brimstone. And the rest were killed with the sword which proceeded from the mouth of Him who sat on the horse. And all the birds were filled with their flesh (Revelation 19:11–21).

83

Who Is the Sheep and Goat Judgment for?

Is the Sheep and Goat Judgment one of nations or individuals?

—Lisa

In Matthew chapter 24, Jesus talks about the End Times. In Matthew chapter 25, He talks about three judgments that will occur when He returns:

- The Wise and Foolish Virgins (10 Virgins) (vv. 1–13)
- The Parable of the Talents (vv. 14–29)
- The Sheep and Goat Judgment (vv. 31–46).

Jesus opens the description of the Sheep and Goat Judgment with these words:

> When the Son of Man comes in His glory, and all the holy angels with Him, then He will sit on the throne of His glory. All the nations will be gathered before Him, and He will separate them one from another, as a shepherd divides *his* sheep from the goats (Matthew 25:31–32).

This judgment will happen just after the Second Coming and before the Millennium. While it is called the Judgment of the *Nations*, it is actually a judgment of individual Gentiles. When Jesus says nations will be gathered to Him, the Greek word translated "nation" is *ethnos* from which we get the words *ethnic* and *ethnicity*. It is simply a reference to ethnic groups. Jesus will bring all the ethnic groups of the world before Him. He does not necessarily mean American, Canadian, French, or German, for example. It means all the ethnicities of the world will be gathered before

Him. Then He will separate them one from another—not nations but individuals. These are Gentiles who were not raptured but survived the Tribulation.

Then Jesus says,

> Then the King will say to those on His right hand, "Come, you blessed of My Father, inherit the kingdom prepared for you from the foundation of the world: for I was hungry and you gave Me food; I was thirsty and you gave Me drink; I was a stranger and you took Me in; I *was* naked and you clothed Me; I was sick and you visited Me; I was in prison and you came to Me."
>
> Then the righteous will answer Him, saying, Lord, when did we see You hungry and feed *You*, or thirsty and give *You* drink? When did we see You a stranger and take *You* in, or naked and clothe *You*? Or when did we see You sick, or in prison, and come to You? And the King will answer and say to them, "Assuredly, I say to you, inasmuch as you did *it* to one of the least of these My brethren, you did *it* to Me" (Matthew 25:34–40).

Jesus is saying when the earth was going through difficulty, how did all these individuals act toward "the least of these My brethren"? There are two ways to interpret that phrase: either He means the Jewish people or the Jewish people plus Christians. I believe Jesus is specifically referring to the Jewish people. When the Jews were being persecuted by the Antichrist and all the nations of the earth turned against them, how did these individuals treat them? Remember, the nations of the world, under the Antichrist, have just waged an all-out war against Israel at the Battle of Armageddon. Jesus says their treatment of the Jews equates to their treatment of Him: "I saw the way that you took care of the Jewish people." He may also be talking about Christians because they will also be severely persecuted during that time.

Jesus will then make the invitation for those who treated "the least of these" well to "come, you blessed of My Father, inherit the kingdom" (v. 34). He is talking about His Millennial Kingdom:

> Then He will also say to those on the left hand, "Depart from Me, you cursed, into the everlasting fire prepared for the devil and his angels: for I was hungry and you gave Me no food; I was thirsty and you gave Me no drink; I was a stranger and you did not take Me in, naked and you did not clothe Me, sick and in prison and you did not visit Me."

Then they also will answer Him, saying, "Lord, when did we see You hungry or thirsty or a stranger or naked or sick or in prison, and did not minister to You?" Then He will answer them, saying, "Assuredly, I say to you, inasmuch as you did not do *it* to one of the least of these, you did not do *it* to Me." And these will go away into everlasting punishment, but the righteous into eternal life (Matthew 25:41–46).

My point here is the way we treat people matters. God takes it personally. Especially the way we treat Jews and the nation of Israel matters to God. You cannot disassociate the way you treat other people, especially Jewish people, from your relationship with God.

In the story of the Sheep and Goat Judgment, both the sheep and goats were surprised that Jesus equated the way they treated "the least of these" with how they treated Him. But He did! Jesus told both the sheep and goats that they were being rewarded or punished because He had seen the way they were treating His brethren and took it personally. So we all need to remember to be careful how we treat everyone but especially the Jewish people.

Questions About ...

Jesus' Second Coming and the Millennium

After Jesus returns, the Antichrist and the False Prophet will be thrown alive into the lake of fire, and Satan will be bound in the bottomless pit for a thousand years. Then what happens? During that time, believers will rule with Jesus over the earth and the people in it. There will be millions or perhaps billions of people who survive the Tribulation.

As it is right now, we are not able to rule the way God intended. The purpose of the Millennial Reign is that for 1,000 years the world will be under Jesus' total control and authority. Those of us who are believers will be "God's Will Enforcement Officers," directly under the authority of Jesus Himself.

Maybe you are looking at what you see in the world right now just as I am. We see evil and immorality all around us. We pray for God to intervene, and sometimes He does. Other times, He gives us the grace to endure it. Here is the good news: Jesus Christ will rule and reign for a thousand years, and we will be by His side.

84

Will Demons Be Bound with Satan?

Will all demons be confined to the abyss with Satan at the beginning of the Millennial Reign? Will they also be freed with Satan at the end?

—Doug

If you read a headline during World War II that said, "Hitler Has Been Bound," then Hitler had been restrained, but the Nazis would also be restrained. So I think at the beginning of the Millennium, when Satan is bound, it can be inferred that the demons are bound with him. This is how the apostle John describes this event in the book of Revelation:

> Then I saw an angel coming down from heaven, having the key to the bottomless pit and a great chain in his hand. He laid hold of the dragon, that serpent of old, who is *the* devil and Satan, and bound him for a thousand years; and he cast him into the bottomless pit, and shut him up, and set a seal on him, so that he should deceive the nations no more till the thousand years were finished. But after these things he must be released for a little while (20:1–3).

The Bible doesn't describe the location of the demons after Satan is bound, so I don't know where they will be, but I believe they will not be active. During the Millennial Reign, Jesus will rule the earth with complete authority. There will be no demonic presence on the earth. It makes sense that they would be bound with Satan. However, Scripture does not explicitly say what God will do with them. But I am certain they will be inactive. Satan, their boss, will be locked up with no escape. I believe they will probably be locked up with him. This would also include the fallen angels spoken about in Jude 6 and 2 Peter 2:4.

In the Millennium, the blessing of God will return to the earth. For example, people will have very long lifespans. The prophet Isaiah says,

> No more shall an infant from there *live but a few* days,
> Nor an old man who has not fulfilled his days;
> For the child shall die one hundred years old,
> But the sinner *being* one hundred years old shall be accursed
> (Isaiah 65:20).

If a person dies at only 100 years of age, everyone will think of them as a just a child and accursed. The earth will also be blessed. The wolf will dwell with the lamb. A child will play next to a serpent's den (Isaiah 11:6–9).

So during the Millennium there will be no space for any demonic activity whatsoever. It will be a wonderful existence with Jesus Christ as our Lord. We will be in our resurrected, new bodies with no sin nature. There will also be no Satan or demons, but when Satan is loosed at the end of the thousand years, he will come back with a vengeance to make his last stand. His deception will cover the earth. Finally, God will put him down for all time, and Satan will never again return to bother humanity.

85

What Happens to Us in the Millennium?

Could you explain more about the Millennial Reign? Will we live on earth similar to the way we live now? Will we be married or have children or jobs?

—Marixa

It will be radically different during the Millennium. First, we will have new supernatural and supranatural bodies. We will be part of nature, yet our bodies will be above nature. We will have no sin nature. We will be glorious and immortal. According to 1 Corinthians chapter 15, our corruptible bodies will put on incorruption (vv. 53–54).

During the Millennium, we will definitely not live the way we do right now. We will never sin again, of course. During the Millennium, Satan and the demons will be locked up in the bottomless pit. We will be ruling and reigning with Jesus. We will actually be a part of the government of Jesus Christ.

This is Revelation chapter 20:

> And I saw thrones, and they sat on them, and judgment was committed to them. Then *I saw* the souls of those who had been beheaded for their witness to Jesus and for the word of God, who had not worshiped the beast or his image, and had not received *his* mark on their foreheads or on their hands. And they lived and reigned with Christ for a thousand years. But the rest of the dead did not live again until the thousand years were finished. This *is* the first resurrection (vv. 4–5).

In Revelation chapter 1, we read that God has made us kings and priests in Jesus:

Grace to you and peace from Him who is and who was and who is to come, and from the seven Spirits who are before His throne, and from Jesus Christ, the faithful witness, the firstborn from the dead, and the ruler over the kings of the earth.

To Him who loved us and washed us from our sins in His own blood, and has made us kings and priests to His God and Father, to Him *be* glory and dominion forever and ever. Amen. (vv. 4–6).

We are kings and priests who reign with Christ for a thousand years.

It's hard in this lifetime. Right now, if you are a teacher, a lawyer, or police officer, then it will not be that way in the Millennium. In fact, in this world, Christians are in the minority, and we're being oppressed and persecuted. In the Millennium, we will be a part of the reign of Jesus Christ over the entire earth. We are the governors and co-regents on earth serving Jesus.

In terms of family, I think we will be very close to our family members who are there with us. By that, I mean our saved loved ones—spouses, children, parents, siblings, grandparents, or other family members. I believe God will group people into families. I believe that because God is a family kind of a God, so I think we will all have family there. I believe we will have tremendous relationships without conflict or disappointment.

There will be no sickness, death, sorrow, or loss. We will never be bored. In the Millennial Reign of Christ, we will have tremendous amounts to do serving and worshipping Jesus and being priests and kings on the earth. It will be an extremely exciting time.

As far as children are concerned, our family members who are saved today will be with us, but we won't be having children. Once we are in our eternal state, I don't believe we will procreate. Procreation on this earth is simply for the purpose of building a family for God. His family is so important to Him that He was willing to give Jesus to die for our sins. However, in the Millennium and in Heaven, we will not be having new babies (see Matthew 22:30).

86

Who Will Reign with Jesus?

If so many people die during the seven years of the Tribulation, and those who did not take the Mark of the Beast are raptured at the end of those years, who will be left for the 1,000-year reign? Who will reign with Jesus?
—Cheryl

This is from Revelation chapter 20:

> And I saw thrones, and they sat on them, and judgment was committed to them. Then I *saw* the souls of those who had been beheaded for their witness to Jesus and for the word of God, who had not worshiped the beast or his image, and had not received *his* mark on their foreheads or on their hands. And they lived and reigned with Christ for a thousand years. But the rest of the dead did not live again until the thousand years were finished. This *is* the first resurrection. Blessed and holy *is* he who has part in the first resurrection. Over such the second death has no power, but they shall be priests of God and of Christ, and shall reign with Him a thousand years (vv. 4–6).

According to the story of the Sheep and Goat Judgment in Matthew chapter 25, the only survivors of the Tribulation are the Sheep nations. Here is that story:

> When the Son of Man comes in His glory, and all the holy angels with Him, then He will sit on the throne of His glory. All the nations will be gathered before Him, and He will separate them one from another, as a shepherd divides *his* sheep from the goats. And He will set the sheep on His right hand, but the goats on the left. Then the King will say to those on His right hand, "Come, you blessed of My Father, inherit the kingdom prepared for you from the foundation of the world: for I was hungry and you gave Me food; I was thirsty and you gave Me drink; I was a stranger and you took Me in; I *was* naked and you clothed Me; I was sick and you visited Me; I was in prison and you came to Me."

Then the righteous will answer Him, saying, "Lord, when did we see You hungry and feed *You*, or thirsty and give *You* drink? When did we see You a stranger and take *You* in, or naked and clothe *You?* Or when did we see You sick, or in prison, and come to You?" And the King will answer and say to them, "Assuredly, I say to you, inasmuch as you did *it* to one of the least of these My brethren, you did *it* to Me."

Then He will also say to those on the left hand, "Depart from Me, you cursed, into the everlasting fire prepared for the devil and his angels: for I was hungry and you gave Me no food; I was thirsty and you gave Me no drink; I was a stranger and you did not take Me in, naked and you did not clothe Me, sick and in prison and you did not visit Me."

Then they also will answer Him, saying, "Lord, when did we see You hungry or thirsty or a stranger or naked or sick or in prison, and did not minister to You?" Then He will answer them, saying, "Assuredly, I say to you, inasmuch as you did not do *it* to one of the least of these, you did not do *it* to Me." And these will go away into everlasting punishment, but the righteous into eternal life (vv. 31–46).

The Sheep and Goat Judgment occurs at the end of the Tribulation and before the Millennium begins. The word "nation" used in this text is the Greek word *ethnos*, from which we get our English word *ethnic*. In the text in Matthew 25, it doesn't mean nations like the United States, France, China, or others. It means all of the different kinds of people in the world.

The Sheep and Goat Judgment is one of individual Gentiles (non-Jews) and how they treated "the least of these My brethren" during the Tribulation. I believe the "least of these" Jesus is talking about are the Jewish people and Israel because He refers to them as "My brethren." But it could also include how people treated believers.

At the end of the judgment, the goat nations are sentenced to Hell. But the sheep nations are welcomed into the Kingdom of God. The interesting thing about this is that there is no reference to them being changed or immortalized. Therefore, they enter into the Millennium in their mortal bodies. As mortals, they will also be procreating during the Millennium. The Bible has a number of references to babies and children during the Millennium, such as:

The wolf also shall dwell with the lamb,
The leopard shall lie down with the young goat,
The calf and the young lion and the fatling together;

And a little child shall lead them.
The cow and the bear shall graze;
Their young ones shall lie down together;
And the lion shall eat straw like the ox.
The nursing child shall play by the cobra's hole,
And the weaned child shall put his hand in the viper's den.
They shall not hurt nor destroy in all My holy mountain,
For the earth shall be full of the knowledge of the LORD
As the waters cover the sea (Isaiah 11:6–9).

The only reasonable conclusion is that those who are blessed by Jesus and welcomed into the Millennial Kingdom are still mortal and are having children during the Millennium. No one else has survived the Tribulation. Therefore, those we are reigning over during the Millennium are the blessed "sheep" people and their offspring.

Remember, we are not mortals during the Millennium. We have physical bodies, but they are immortal, incorruptible, and glorious. We have no sin nature, and we have the full authority of our Husband, Jesus. The mortals on the earth and the earth itself are all under our authority. As the mortals on the earth multiply for 1,000 years, not all of their offspring desire to follow Jesus or be under His authority. This is obvious through this text that records the events on the earth at the end of the Millennium:

Now when the thousand years have expired, Satan will be released from his prison and will go out to deceive the nations which are in the four corners of the earth, Gog and Magog, to gather them together to battle, whose number *is* as the sand of the sea. They went up on the breadth of the earth and surrounded the camp of the saints and the beloved city. And fire came down from God out of heaven and devoured them. The devil, who deceived them, was cast into the lake of fire and brimstone where the beast and the false prophet *are*. And they will be tormented day and night forever and ever (Revelation 20:7–10).

It is hard to believe that people who have lived under the perfect rule of Jesus for hundreds of years would then reject Him, but they do. When the devil is released, he has little problem finding rebels to join him in his pathetic final attempt to defeat the Son of God. And that is the final scene that ends world history as we know it.

87

Will People Die in the Millennium?

Will the curse of Adam and Eve still rest on humanity during the Millennial Reign? And will people die during this time?

—Tabitha

Concerning those who have been married to Jesus at the Marriage Supper of the Lamb, there will be no curse. According to Revelation chapter 19, we will have been perfected. We will already be the wife of Jesus Christ and return with Him at the Second Coming. We will then rule and reign with Him for a thousand years. Since we will be perfected, it will not be possible for us to sin. Jesus will remove our sin nature and every curse that comes with it.

There will also be a removal of the curse on the earth. During the Millennium, the earth will become a paradise as God originally created it to be, and the mortals on the earth will live unusually long lives. Here is a picture of that time from the prophet Isaiah:

"No more shall an infant from there *live but a few* days,
Nor an old man who has not fulfilled his days;
For the child shall die one hundred years old,
But the sinner *being* one hundred years old shall be accursed.
They shall build houses and inhabit *them*;
They shall plant vineyards and eat their fruit.
They shall not build and another inhabit;
They shall not plant and another eat;
For as the days of a tree, *so shall be* the days of My people,
And My elect shall long enjoy the work of their hands.
They shall not labor in vain,
Nor bring forth children for trouble;

For they *shall be* the descendants of the blessed of the LORD,
And their offspring with them.
It shall come to pass
That before they call, I will answer;
And while they are still speaking, I will hear.
The wolf and the lamb shall feed together,
The lion shall eat straw like the ox,
And dust *shall be* the serpent's food.
They shall not hurt nor destroy in all My holy mountain,"
Says the Lord (Isaiah 65:20–25).

You can see from the above passage that during the Millennium mortals are still dying, but they are living unusually long lives: "For as the days of a tree, so shall be the days of My people" (v. 22).

But there is a text in Zechariah that tells us the mortals remaining on the earth after the Tribulation must worship the Lord, or they will suffer serious consequences:

> And it shall come to pass *that* everyone who is left of all the nations which came against Jerusalem shall go up from year to year to worship the King, the LORD of hosts, and to keep the Feast of Tabernacles. And it shall be *that* whichever of the families of the earth do not come up to Jerusalem to worship the King, the LORD of hosts, on them there will be no rain. If the family of Egypt will not come up and enter in, they *shall have* no *rain*; they shall receive the plague with which the LORD strikes the nations who do not come up to keep the Feast of Tabernacles. This shall be the punishment of Egypt and the punishment of all the nations that do not come up to keep the Feast of Tabernacles.
>
> In that day "HOLINESS TO THE LORD" shall be *engraved* on the bells of the horses. The pots in the LORD's house shall be like the bowls before the altar. Yes, every pot in Jerusalem and Judah shall be holiness to the LORD of hosts. Everyone who sacrifices shall come and take them and cook in them. In that day there shall no longer be a Canaanite in the house of the LORD of hosts (14:16–21).

The Millennium for believers will be a time of incredible blessing as we rule and reign with Jesus for one thousand years in our perfected bodies. But for the mortals living on the earth, there will be a time of unprecedented peace, beauty, longevity, and abundance—provided they are obedient to the Lord and His commands.

88

Can We Travel to Heaven in the Millennium?

As we reign with Jesus during the Millennium, will we be able to go back and forth to Heaven during that prolonged period of time? If not, wouldn't we be disappointed after getting a seven-year experience of Heaven only to return to earth for 1,000 years?

—Renee

That is a really good question. During the seven years of the Tribulation, believers who have died or gone with Jesus at the Rapture will celebrating with Jesus at the Marriage Supper of the Lamb. The bride of Christ will become the wife of Christ. Revelation chapters 21 and 22 describe what this exquisite place called the Father's house will be like.

So yes, we will be at the Father's house for seven years. You are also correct that we will come back with Jesus at the Second Coming. The Millennium will begin, and we will rule and reign with Jesus for a thousand years. I am confident that our experience won't bring any disappointment. I can promise you that. We will not be disappointed when we see Jesus. We will not be dismayed that we are spending a thousand years with Him.

Now I will give my personal opinion. I cannot prove this through Scripture, but this is what I believe. I believe we will have access to the Father's house during the Millennium. Remember, we will now be in our supernatural, redeemed bodies. We will have no sin nature. I believe we will have the ability to travel at the speed of thought. You could be on the earth ruling and reigning with Jesus one minute and beam up for lunch or something like that in Heaven the next. So yes, I believe will have access to our eternal home. Again, it is my opinion, but I hope it happens that way.

89

Why Will Satan Be Released Again?

After the 1,000-year reign of Jesus and the saints, why is the devil released to corrupt the world again?
—Browning

I believe God will release the devil to prove people's hearts. Even though the sheep nations were blessed by Jesus in Matthew chapter 25 and allowed to enter the Millennial Kingdom, their offspring will also have to make their choice regarding Jesus. At the end of the Millennium, the earth is full of the descendants of the sheep nations. And they have had to live under the iron rod rule of Jesus for 1,000 years.

You might think that everyone would love to be under Jesus' perfect rule, but you would be wrong. At the end of the Millennium when Satan is released for a short period of time, he will go into the world to deceive the nations into rebelling against Jesus and us. Unfortunately, he will have great success. Here is that account:

> Now when the thousand years have expired, Satan will be released from his prison and will go out to deceive the nations which are in the four corners of the earth, Gog and Magog, to gather them together to battle, whose number *is* as the sand of the sea. They went up on the breadth of the earth and surrounded the camp of the saints and the beloved city. And fire came down from God out of heaven and devoured them. The devil, who deceived them, was cast into the lake of fire and brimstone where the beast and the false prophet *are*. And they will be tormented day and night forever and ever (Revelation 20:7–10).

This is a time of proving for the world before God destroys the heavens and the earth and creates new ones. He will not allow rebellion in Heaven, so everyone has to make a choice to serve

Him or reject Him. That is why I believe Satan is released at the end of the Millennium. Just as he did in the Garden of Eden with Adam and Eve, he acts as an agent of division. Will we serve God or rebel against Him? Will we submit or refuse? Will we accept our humble state or rise up in prideful defiance? That is a decision all of us have to make, and it will be no different for those mortals in the Millennium.

Questions About ...

God's Final Triumph

As humans, we have lived on this planet for a long time, yet for the most part, we have forgotten who we are. God created us as the kings of the earth. He made us to be His priests. He called us to be a royal priesthood. But sin has corrupted our hearts and clouded our minds.

God has given us spiritual authority. We can rule right now with the Holy Spirit's empowerment. We often forget we have that power. God is going to finally triumph over all evil. He will finally control everything. When Jesus gives us life again beyond this world, we will have total authority, and we won't forget it. We will reign with Him as kings. He always intended to give us dominion, and as the wife of Jesus Christ, we will finally recognize it and live according to it.

When we go to Heaven, God will transform everything about us. We won't age, get sick, or grieve. Everyone in Heaven will finally be fully matured, totally healthy, and in eternal, glorified bodies. It is beyond anything we can imagine.

90

Will We Have Free Will in Heaven?

Since Satan was an angel and had free will, when we are in Heaven, will we still have free will?

—Caroline

Yes, we will still have free will, but we will no longer have a sin nature. We have already chosen Jesus, so we're never going to use our will against Him again.

According to Isaiah chapter 14 and Ezekiel chapter 28, God created Satan as Lucifer in a place called "Eden, the garden of God" (Ezekiel 28:13). He was a covering cherub and had musical instruments built into his body. He was a worship leader in Heaven in the presence of God. And he had free will. All the angels did. Then a third of the angels joined with Lucifer in a rebellion against God according to Revelation chapter 12. So he had a free will but chose to exalt himself above God. God cast him down for the rebellion. Satan didn't have a sin nature, but he still sinned.

The second garden was the Garden of Eden, and God created Adam and Eve. They also did not have a sin nature, but Satan came and tempted them. They followed him into sin and lost that garden paradise. So the first paradise was with God in eternity past. It was spoiled by Satan's rebellion. The second paradise was in the Garden of Eden, and Adam and Even spoiled it with their rebellion.

The third garden Paradise is where we are going with Jesus. It is the New Jerusalem we read about Revelation chapters 21 and 22. Those two chapters give a very graphic and detailed description. No one is born or created there. Everyone there chooses to go. Satan did not choose Heaven. God created him perfect, but God chose him for it. Adam and Eve did not choose the Garden of

Eden. God created them in it even though they rebelled against Him after He did. In spite of everything God did for them, they were unappreciative and traded God for a piece of fruit. However, every person in Heaven, the final Paradise, will have a free will, but it will not be used against God. We will have chosen to be there. It is important to choose Christ. We will still have free will, but we will use it to freely love and serve the One who died for us.

91

Can People in Hell Change
Their Minds?

**Does Satan have authority over people in Hell? Is Hell
a place of torture or of darkness and loneliness? When
Jesus returns, are people who are already in Hell allowed
to change their minds and go to Heaven?**

—Howard

First, Satan has absolutely no authority. Jesus said, "All authority
has been given to Me in heaven and on earth" (Matthew 28:18).
So Satan will have zero authority in Hell. I once heard a guy say, "I
don't want to go to Heaven. I want to go to Hell 'cause I'm going
to party with the devil." I can assure you there will be no partying
in Hell. Satan has no authority there. He will be under judgment.
This is what John wrote about Hell:

> Then a third angel followed them, saying with a loud voice, "If any-
> one worships the beast and his image, and receives *his* mark on his
> forehead or on his hand, he himself shall also drink of the wine of the
> wrath of God, which is poured out full strength into the cup of His
> indignation. He shall be tormented with fire and brimstone in the
> presence of the holy angels and in the presence of the Lamb. And the
> smoke of their torment ascends forever and ever; and they have no
> rest day or night, who worship the beast and his image, and whoever
> receives the mark of his name" (Revelation 14:9–11).

That certainly does not sound like the description of a party. Hell
will be torment in the presence of the angels and Jesus. Only Jesus
is Lord of Hell. The demons will never be over Hell; the Lord is.

When Jesus returns, the people in Hell will not have another
opportunity to receive Jesus. On the cross, Jesus was crucified
between two thieves. One thief mocked Him. But the other thief

humbly asked Jesus to remember him when Jesus received His Kingdom. Jesus promised the man they would be in Paradise together that very day. We have an eternal choice. There is a heresy that teaches ultimate reconciliation with a type of purgatory even for unbelievers to repent after death. They teach some people will go to Hell for a certain period of time depending upon how bad they were on earth. Then after a time of purification, they will be allowed into Heaven. According to this line of thought, Adolf Hitler will ultimately be up in Heaven with Abraham. That is not what the Bible teaches—*anywhere*.

Hell is forever. The fire will never go out. Revelation chapter 14 says the smoke of their torment goes up forever. I do believe there are levels of Hell. I think Satan will obviously be in the very lowest pit of Hell. Jesus said of Bethsaida and Capernaum, the area where He lived and performed a lot of His miracles, that it will be better on the day of judgment for Sodom and Gomorrah than for those two cities. He said this because they had seen Him perform many miracles and still did not repent (Matthew 11:21). Even though there are levels, there's no good place in Hell. It is an eternal place of darkness and torment.

Some people wonder why a loving God would send anyone to Hell. A loving God sent Jesus to die for our sins so we don't have to go to Hell. Why would anyone turn down the free gift of Jesus? That's the real question. Who would turn away the grace of Jesus? However, Jesus knew many people would still reject Him. Here is what He said about it:

> And this is the condemnation, that the light has come into the world, and men loved darkness rather than light, because their deeds were evil (John 3:19).

Many people won't come to Jesus because they don't want their deeds exposed. Others come to Him because they love Him and want Him. The penalty for rejecting Jesus is eternity in Hell. That's why Jesus said,

> If your right eye causes you to sin, pluck it out and cast *it* from you; for it is more profitable for you that one of your members perish, than

for your whole body to be cast into hell. And if your right hand causes you to sin, cut it off and cast *it* from you; for it is more profitable for you that one of your members perish, than for your whole body to be cast into hell (Matthew 5:29–30).

92

What Will Happen to the Unsaved Killed at the Second Coming?

After the Second Coming of Jesus, when Satan and the Antichrist are thrown alive into the lake of fire, it says that those who did not get saved are killed with the sword. So do they not spend eternity in Hell?

—April

Satan will not be thrown into the lake of fire yet when Jesus returns. However, it will be the False Prophet and the Antichrist who are cast alive into the lake of fire. Satan will be bound in the bottomless pit for a thousand years. All those events are described in Revelation chapter 20.

Everyone who is not saved will go to Hell. Unbelieving people who are killed when Jesus returns will be brought back to life at the end of the Millennium for the Great White Throne Judgment. After that, they will be sent to Hell (Revelation 20).

93

Are the Dead Sleeping Until the Rapture?

I have many friends and family in Heaven. I would love to know what they're doing. I know the Bible says they are asleep in Jesus, but are they just sleeping until the Rapture? Or are they worshipping God and in fellowship with those who have gone before them?

—Luana

Paul says,

> But I do not want you to be ignorant, brethren, concerning those who have fallen asleep, lest you sorrow as others who have no hope. For if we believe that Jesus died and rose again, even so God will bring with Him those who sleep in Jesus (1 Thessalonians 4:13–14).

The word translated "sleep" in these verses simply means "to lie down" in Greek. It is unfortunate that some people have built a whole doctrine around "soul sleep" when that is not what these verses are teaching. Paul was using a Greek idiom or euphemism about death. We might say someone has "passed away." If we take those words literally, someone might think we mean someone simply traveled to another town. We really mean they have died. The people Paul is writing about have been laid down in the tomb—but they are not sleeping. Look at what Jesus said to Martha about death:

> Jesus said to her, "Your brother will rise again."
> Martha said to Him, "I know that he will rise again in the resurrection at the last day."
> Jesus said to her, "I am the resurrection and the life. **He who believes in Me, though he may die, he shall live. And whoever lives and believes in Me shall never die.** Do you believe this?" (John 11:23–26, bold mine).

237

To the thief on the cross, Jesus said, "Assuredly, I say to you, today you will be with Me in Paradise" (Luke 23:43). So Christians never die. Jesus said, "And whoever lives and believes in Me shall never die" (John 11:25). This is not soul sleep. Jesus told the thief they would be in Paradise together *that* day.

I think Don Piper has given one of the most credible accounts of Heaven in his book *90 Minutes in Heaven*. Don clinically died, went to Heaven, and came back. He was dead for 90 minutes. When he went to Heaven, he saw relatives and friends. Everyone was alive. He wrote about phenomenal colors, tastes, and smells. His account is consistent with other people who have had the same experience. He said Heaven was the most incredible thing he had ever seen. People were loving each other and incredibly happy.

So I absolutely believe Christians who die are fellowshipping with one another. They love each other. They are worshipping Jesus and are in His presence. They are enjoying all the blessings of Heaven. I do not believe at all that we will go into some sort of a soul sleep. Paul simply uses an idiom for the fact that bodies are laid down in the grave.

94

Who Will Be Judged at the Great White Throne?

If the Great White Throne Judgment is for all non-believers, pre-Messiah, and post-Messiah, then why is there a separation of sheep and goats? Won't all unbelievers go to Hell?

—Hollis

All unbelievers will go to hell. But the sheep nations, the individual sheep people, are believers. This is what Jesus says about the people He calls sheep:

> When the Son of Man comes in His glory, and all the holy angels with Him, then He will sit on the throne of His glory. All the nations will be gathered before Him, and He will separate them one from another, as a shepherd divides *his* sheep from the goats. And He will set the sheep on His right hand, but the goats on the left. Then the King will say to those on His right hand, "Come, you blessed of My Father, inherit the kingdom prepared for you from the foundation of the world: for I was hungry and you gave Me food; I was thirsty and you gave Me drink; I was a stranger and you took Me in; I *was* naked and you clothed Me; I was sick and you visited Me; I was in prison and you came to Me" (Matthew 25:31–36).

So the individuals from the sheep nations will be welcomed into the Kingdom. This event is at the end of the Tribulation. These are the people who have survived the Tribulation. They're in their mortal bodies. They are those who have shown kindness to Israel and the Jews and possibly Christians.

The goats are sent to Hell, but the sheep will be saved. The sheep will come into the Kingdom prepared for them. But they are still in their mortal bodies. They will live as mortals through the Millennium.

The Great White Throne Judgment is for all unbelievers, while the sheep in Matthew chapter 25 are believers. The Great White Throne is a judgment of condemnation for those in rebellion against God. The judgment of Christians will have already occurred. When believers are judged, the righteousness of Jesus covers our sins and presents us blameless before God the Father. God will give us perfect bodies and reward us for the good deeds we have done while we were on earth. The Great White Throne Judgment, however, is for those who are unbelieving and unsaved. These people will spend eternity in Hell. John provides this vision:

> Then I saw a great white throne and Him who sat on it, from whose face the earth and the heaven fled away. And there was found no place for them. And I saw the dead, small and great, standing before God, and books were opened. And another book was opened, which is *the Book* of Life. And the dead were judged according to their works, by the things which were written in the books. The sea gave up the dead who were in it, and Death and Hades delivered up the dead who were in them. And they were judged, each one according to his works. Then Death and Hades were cast into the lake of fire. This is the second death. And anyone not found written in the Book of Life was cast into the lake of fire (Revelation 20:11–15).

At this point, God is finished with this earth as we know it. The final event that will happen is God's creation of a New Heaven and a New Earth.

95

What Is the Purpose of the New Heaven and New Earth?

What is the purpose of the New Heaven? If we are eternally with God and He is creating the New Earth, then will we be able to go between those two places? Is the New Heaven just the sky?

—Aaron

The purpose of the New Heaven and New Earth is purity. Creation was ruined and corrupted because of sin (Romans 8:20–22). Satan rebelled against God in Heaven in eternity past (Isaiah 14:12–17; Ezekiel 28:16). The earth was void and formless, and Satan came and ushered in rebellion with Adam and Eve. There probably aren't many places on earth where something sinful has not taken place. So the heavens and the earth have been corrupted by Satan and fallen humans.

And when Jesus comes again at the Great White Throne Judgment, all of human history will be finished. In triumph, God is going to create a New Heaven and New Earth. On the New Earth, there will not be one place where a sin has ever been committed. There will never be a bad memory or a bad event anywhere on the earth. It's going to be a phenomenal place. The same is true of the New Heaven. There won't be anywhere there that Satan or an evil spirit has ever been. That means there won't be a trace of rebellion and sin in it, and it will be eternal and incorruptible.

I personally believe the New Heaven will be an eternal playground. We will have new bodies and be able to travel at the speed of thought. I believe we will play among the stars and the planets.

Some people believe in a boring Heaven. I believe in a Heaven that is incredible—that eye has not seen, and ear has not heard, nor has it entered into the heart of man what God has prepared for those who love Him (1 Corinthians 2:9). At God's right hand are pleasures forevermore. We will have access to every place we want to go. It will be a place of purity, safety, and wonder, like we've never seen before.

96

Where Is Heaven?

The Rapture takes place in the clouds where Jesus will meet us, but where is Heaven? Is it in the clouds, above the satellites, and further than the moon?

—Paul

This is what Paul says about Heaven:

> I know a man in Christ who fourteen years ago—whether in the body I do not know, or whether out of the body I do not know, God knows—such a one was caught up to the third heaven. And I know such a man—whether in the body or out of the body I do not know, God knows—how he was caught up into Paradise and heard inexpressible words, which it is not lawful for a man to utter (2 Corinthians 12:2–4).

So when Paul refers to the third Heaven, what does that mean? The first heaven is the atmosphere around the earth. The second heaven is what we would refer to as outer space. The third Heaven is the presence of God.

So where is Heaven? I have no idea. Is it in the universe? Is it outside the universe? Is it a spiritual dimension, or is it physical also? There are many questions about Heaven we just don't have the answers to. But it is real, and it is where God dwells with His people.

Understand that when Jesus returns for us, we will marry Him in the Father's house as described in Revelation chapters 21 and 22. That this is where we will spend eternity with Jesus Christ.

I can't tell you exactly where it is, but it is both a physical and spiritual place. Ultimately, the Father's house will come down out of Heaven to a recreated earth, and that is where we will live for all eternity.

How Old Will We Be in Heaven?

How old will we all be in our new redeemed, raptured, and glorified bodies? If we will "be like Christ," then does that mean we will all be 33 years old? What about babies or young children? Will they be in immature bodies for all eternity?
—Richie

Time is a prison, but God is not imprisoned by it. He is eternal and transcendent. Time does not apply to God, except He is aware that it applies to us. He is not in time. Einstein's theory of relativity proves that time and space are created dimensions. If they are created, then there must be a creator, and we know that God is the Creator. He is timeless and will never age as we understand aging. Some people imagine God as old. Nothing could be further from the truth. Even though He is eternal, He is also ageless!

When we go to Heaven, God will transform us into timeless bodies. Age will not apply to us. We will simply be timeless and fully matured. I believe babies and children who died young or who will be raptured will also be fully matured. I don't know how this will happen. It could be instantaneous, or it might happen through a maturation process. Whatever the case, I believe everyone in Heaven will finally be fully matured, totally healthy, and in eternal, glorified bodies.

On my next birthday, I will turn 70. I know the clock is ticking. However, in Heaven, that clock and calendar will not matter at all. You won't turn 39. You won't turn 80. You will be in Heaven trillions and trillions of years, but your body will be exactly the same, and you will have no "body issues." Believe that. You will like your body. It will have no aging. It will be timeless but fully matured and completely healthy. What age will we be? *The perfect age—forever!*

How Will We Travel in Eternity?

How will we travel in Heaven and the New Earth? Will there be vehicles? Will we be teleporting like in virtual reality?

—Ryan

What an interesting question! We are talking about life in Heaven and the New Earth. To understand this issue, we must first recognize that Jesus is the firstfruits of many brethren. This is what Paul says about that:

> But now Christ is risen from the dead, *and* has become the firstfruits of those who have fallen asleep. For since by man *came* death, by Man also *came* the resurrection of the dead. For as in Adam all die, even so in Christ all shall be made alive. But each one in his own order: Christ the firstfruits, afterward those *who are* Christ's at His coming (1 Corinthians 15:20–23).

What happened to Jesus in His resurrection will also happen to us in the Rapture or if we die before and are resurrected.

After Jesus was resurrected, He met two of His followers on the road to Emmaus. When they arrived, the followers asked Jesus to stay with them. They talked about Jesus being crucified in Jerusalem, but the followers did not recognize Him. They sat down to eat, and this is what happened:

> Now it came to pass, as He sat at the table with them, that He took bread, blessed and broke *it*, and gave it to them. Then their eyes were opened and they knew Him; and He vanished from their sight (Luke 24:30–31).

Then Jesus appeared to the disciples on the Mount of Olives, and He ascended into Heaven without the protection of a spacesuit (see Acts 1:9). Therefore, I don't believe there will be vehicles in

Heaven or in the New Earth. We won't need them. I believe that we will be able to travel at the speed of thought. Just think and you can go from one place to another. That's what Jesus did.

We are locked in three dimensions right now. In Heaven, we will not be limited by any number of dimensions. We know there are extra dimensions because angels can appear and disappear. We know there's a supernatural realm we can't see. When Elisha asked God to open the eyes of his servant, the servant saw the mountains filled with chariots of fire there to defend them (see 2 Kings 6:8–23). That's an example of a dimension we cannot see.

We are limited in these bodies on this earth. We will be unlimited when we get to Heaven. I can only imagine how amazing it will be. Perhaps there will be vehicles for amusement, but we won't need them for the purpose of getting us from one place to the other. We will be able to do that supernaturally because we will be in our resurrected bodies.

99

What Will Happen with Those Who Have Hurt Us?

How are we supposed to interact with those who have been our abusers in Heaven? Some of them will have repented, so they are able to inherit the Kingdom of God. What will happen when we see them?

—Anna

This is a very thought-provoking question. I have to be honest—I do my very best to follow Jesus, but there are occasionally people who try my patience. I might want to punch them in the nose, but I don't. The truth is there are some people I don't like very much, and there are some who have done me wrong. It's an unpleasant experience to be around them. If I saw them in public, I probably wouldn't go out of my way to greet them or be friendly. I just don't like them for what they have done to me or other people I care about.

The thought of seeing someone in Heaven who has hurt us, especially someone who has sexually assaulted, physically abused, or even murdered us or a loved one, is more than most of us can contemplate. I am reminded, however, that the apostle Paul helped murder Christians before he became a believer. He is in Heaven right now with those people. The deacon Stephen was stoned to death, and Paul watched the coats of those who were throwing rocks. In fact, it was a tradition for the person who threw the first stone to watch the garments of those who finished the execution as a way to show solidarity between all the executioners. I don't know if that is what happened with Paul, but it makes sense. How would you feel if you arrived in Heaven and the person who murdered you showed up? It would be pretty shocking!

One of the thieves crucified next to Jesus turned to him in faith even while they were both on crosses. Jesus told that man they would be together in Paradise that day. Can you imagine seeing a man who robbed you showing up with Jesus in Heaven?

So, yes, this is a difficult question, but there's something wonderful about what is being asked. Thank God we will all be different! It's hard to imagine on this side of Heaven being confronted with the presence of our abusers and seeing the people we really dislike and who have hurt us or our families. There are those who have defrauded, cheated, and betrayed us. Nevertheless, I believe on the other side, we won't have any fleshly thoughts, feelings, or egos. We won't know pain; it will all be resolved:

> And God will wipe away every tear from their eyes; there shall be no more death, nor sorrow, nor crying. There shall be no more pain, for the former things have passed away (Revelation 21:4).

In Heaven, we are brothers and sisters; we are one in Christ. There's no sense of pain. I don't believe there will be bad memories or any animosity. Trust God that He will take care of you, and even though you still feel pain when you think about someone who has hurt you, believe that one day He will make all things new.

100

Does Satan Know
He Will Lose?

The Bible clearly says Satan will ultimately lose, and he knows it. Then why does he still try to outsmart God? Does he think he can turn it around and win?

—Alwynn

Yes, Satan will ultimately lose, but I don't believe he knows it. I don't know where the Bible says that. The End Times will soon reveal the Antichrist—who is Satan incarnate. This evil man will rise to power and ultimately control the entire world. In an act of ultimate pride and deception, he will go into a rebuilt Temple in Jerusalem and proclaim that he is God. This is called the Abomination of Desolation and is described by Daniel, Jesus, Paul, and John.

Satan fell in eternities past by trying to steal the glory from God so he could put his throne above the throne of God. Even though it cost him dearly, he has evidently not learned his lesson. The Antichrist's efforts to proclaim himself God will be just another attempt for Satan to usurp God's glory and try to set his throne above the Lord's.

I believe the devil still thinks he can win. He is that deceived! And his tireless attempts to promote his evil actors into strategic positions for the End Times just tell us he is still sincerely trying to win. Even though I believe Satan knows a lot about the Bible, he doesn't understand it. His mind is darkened. He is totally deceived.

Yes, the Bible clearly reveals the ultimate defeat of Satan. But I don't think he has read that part. And if he has, he clearly doesn't understand it!

A Very Important Question

Are you ready for Jesus' return? Do you want to make sure? I have a very important personal question to ask you. In fact, it is the most important question you will ever be asked to answer:

Have you invited Jesus into your heart to be your Lord and Savior?

If your answer is "no" to that question, then I need to tell you that it is very important for you to invite Jesus into your heart. Unless you surrender to Jesus and have a personal relationship with Him, you will not be ready to meet Him when He comes.

Here are some important Scriptures to help you understand the significance of this major step:

> For by grace you have been saved through faith, and that not of your-selves; *it is* the gift of God, not of works, lest anyone should boast (Ephesians 2:8–9).

> Behold, I stand at the door and knock. If anyone hears My voice and opens the door, I will come in to him and dine with him, and he with Me (Revelation 3:20).

> For God so loved the world that He gave His only begotten Son, that whoever believes in Him should not perish but have everlasting life.

251

For God did not send His Son into the world to condemn the world, but that the world through Him might be saved.

He who believes in Him is not condemned; but he who does not believe is condemned already, because he has not believed in the name of the only begotten Son of God (John 3:16–18).

Salvation (being saved) is an act of grace that we don't deserve. It is a free gift from God that we receive instantly as we open our hearts to Jesus and allow Him into our lives to save us from our sins and become our Lord. God loves you personally and wants to have a personal relationship with you. As you open your heart to Jesus and invite Him in, He will forgive all your sins, give you the gift of eternal life in Heaven forever, live in your heart, and personally relate to you. He will also take you with Him when He comes back to gather His people. He does all this because of His great love for you. This love is not one God has for us because we deserve it. He loves us because He created us in our mothers' wombs (see Psalm 139:13–16), and we are His children, made in His image.

Jesus died for us on the cross to pay for our sins and break the power of sin over our lives. He did this because sin was keeping us away from God, and there was no way we could deal with our sin problem on our own. Knowing that we were helpless in our sins, God sent Jesus, His only Son, to die in our place and pay for our sins so they could be removed forever.

When we receive Jesus into our lives, we are laying claim to the forgiveness, freedom, and blessings for which Jesus died and rose again. All these blessings flow from our personal relationship with Him. If you are ready to receive Jesus into your heart at this time, say this prayer to Him:

> *Jesus, I confess that I have sinned against You, and I repent. I now open my heart to You and ask You to come into my life to be my Lord and Savior. I submit my life to You, and from this day forward I will live to serve You. I believe You have come into my heart and have forgiven me of my sins. I believe I am now saved by Your grace. I have the gift of eternal life, and I am now ready for Your return. Jesus, I pray You will fill me with Your Holy Spirit and give me the power to change, know You, and live my life for You. Amen!*

If you prayed that prayer, then you can be sure that Jesus is now in your heart as the Lord of your life. This is the most important prayer of your life because it changes your eternity. Now, it is also common when you pray this prayer for the devil to try to tell you it isn't real or you are too bad to be forgiven. Don't worry—that happens to almost everyone. Soon you will learn how to discern the voice of the devil and how to overcome him. For now, just know that you are a child of God, a Christian, and a member of God's family. Welcome!

It is important as a new believer to be baptized in water as an act of obedience to Jesus. It is the first thing Jesus commands us to do as new believers as a token of our sincerity and obedience to Him (see Mark 16:15–16; Matthew 28:19–20). If you don't have a home church, then find a Bible-believing church and tell them you would like to be baptized in water. Be committed to church, attend regularly, and get involved. It will be important to your new faith to be around fellow believers who will encourage you in the things of God. You should also get a Bible if you don't already own one and begin to read it daily. Start in the New Testament, and if you are completely unfamiliar with the Bible, then the Gospel of John is a great book to help you understand who Jesus is and how to have a relationship with Him. Be sure to get a Bible translation you can understand. The New Living Translation is a very good Bible version that is understandable and accurate.

Also, I wrote a book called *Ten Steps Toward Christ: Journey to the Heart of God*, specifically for those who have just given their lives to Christ. I encourage you to purchase a copy and read it. It will show you in detail the important steps to living a victorious and fulfilling Christian life. You can get it on xomarriage.com or Amazon.com. Jesus is coming soon, and I am so happy you will be ready to go with Him when He returns.

About the Author

Jimmy Evans is a long-time pastor, Bible teacher, and bestselling author. He is the Founder and President of XO Marriage, a ministry devoted to helping couples thrive in strong and fulfilling marriages. For 30 years, Jimmy ministered as Senior Pastor of Trinity Fellowship Church in Amarillo, Texas, where he now serves as Apostolic Elder. During his time as senior pastor, the church grew from 900 to over 10,000 members. Jimmy loves mentoring pastors and helping local churches grow to reach their potential. He is a popular speaker at churches and leadership conferences across America. Jimmy has written more than 50 books including *Marriage on the Rock, The Four Laws of Love, 21 Day Inner Healing Journey, Look Up!, Tipping Point,* and *Where Are the Missing People?*. Jimmy and Karen have been married for 50 years and have two married children and five grandchildren.